THE WORLD'S WILDEST RIVERS

WHITE WATER

THE WORLD'S WILDEST RIVERS

WHITE WATER

GRAEME ADDISON

Foreword by Ranulph Fiennes

NH
NEW
HOLLAND

First published in 2001 by
New Holland Publishers
London • Cape Town • Sydney • Auckland

86 Edgware Road
London W2 2EA
United Kingdom

80 McKenzie Street
Cape Town 8001
South Africa

14 Aquatic Drive
Frenchs Forest, NSW 2086
Australia

218 Lake Road
Northcote, Auckland
New Zealand

ISBN 1 85974 501 6

PUBLISHER Mariëlle Renssen
COMMISSIONING EDITOR Claudia dos Santos
MANAGING EDITOR Mari Roberts
MANAGING ART EDITOR Peter Bosman
DESIGNER Heather Dittmar
EDITORS Lauren Copley, Mariëlle Renssen
CONSULTANT (UK) Andy Middleton
PICTURE RESEARCHER Sonya Meyer
CARTOGRAPHER John Loubser
PRODUCTION Myrna Collins

Reproduction by
Hirt & Carter (Pty) Ltd, Cape Town
Printed and bound in Singapore by
Tien Wah Press (Pte) Ltd

2 4 6 8 10 9 7 5 3 1

ENDPAPERS: *Water-worn boulder on the Bhagirathi River, a tributary of the Ganges, India.*
HALF TITLE PAGE: *A kayaker portages his craft in the Black Canyon of the Gunnison River, Colorado.*
FULL TITLE PAGE: *Rafters on the Skykomish River, Cascade mountains, Washington, USA.*
LEFT: *Onlookers watch from a suspension bridge as a rafting crew navigates the Sun Kosi River, Nepal.*

CONTENTS

FOREWORD BY RANULPH FIENNES   9

WORLD MAP OF RIVERS   10

SAFETY & GRADING OF RIVERS   13

INTRODUCTION   14
The Inexorable Pull of Whitewater

NORTH AMERICA   26
Tatshenshini and Alsek, Canada/Alaska   28
Salmon, Idaho   34
American, California   36
Colorado, Arizona   38
Ocoee, Tennessee   43
New, West Virginia   45

CENTRAL & SOUTH AMERICA   46
Pacuare, Costa Rica   49
Amazon, Brazil   50
Orinoco, Venezuela   56
Colca, Peru   60
Futaleufu, Chile   64

EUROPE, ASIA MINOR & MIDDLE EAST   66
Pjörsá and Jokulsá á Fjöllum, Iceland   68
Sjoa, Norway   72
Inn, Austria/Switzerland   76
Mreznica, Dobra and Soca, Slovenia and Croatia   81
Jordan, Israel   86
Dez, Iran   89

ASIA, SIBERIA & CHINA   90
Katun and Chuya, Altai Mountains   92

Chatkal and Pskem, Kyrgyzstan   95
Yangtze, China   102

HIMALAYA   104
Kali Gandaki, Nepal   106
Sun Kosi and Dudh Kosi, Nepal   108
Braldu, Pakistan   112
Sutlej, India   117
Tsangpo (Brahmaputra), Tibet   120

THE EAST, AUSTRALIA
& NEW ZEALAND   122
Alas, Sumatra   125
Padas, Borneo   127
Strickland, Papua New Guinea   128
North Johnstone, Australia   130
Franklin, Australia   131
Waikato, New Zealand   133
Clarence, New Zealand   134

AFRICA   138
Nile, Burundi/Ethiopia   140
Congo (Zaïre), Central Africa   142
Zambezi, Zimbabwe   146
Orange, South Africa   150
Tugela, South Africa   153

GLOSSARY   156

REFERENCES AND
FURTHER READING   157

INDEX   158

LEFT: *The oarsman manoeuvres to strike a wall of white water obliquely on the Colorado River, USA.*
FOLLOWING PAGES: *An oared raft batters its way through Rapid No. 7, Zambezi River, Southern Africa.*

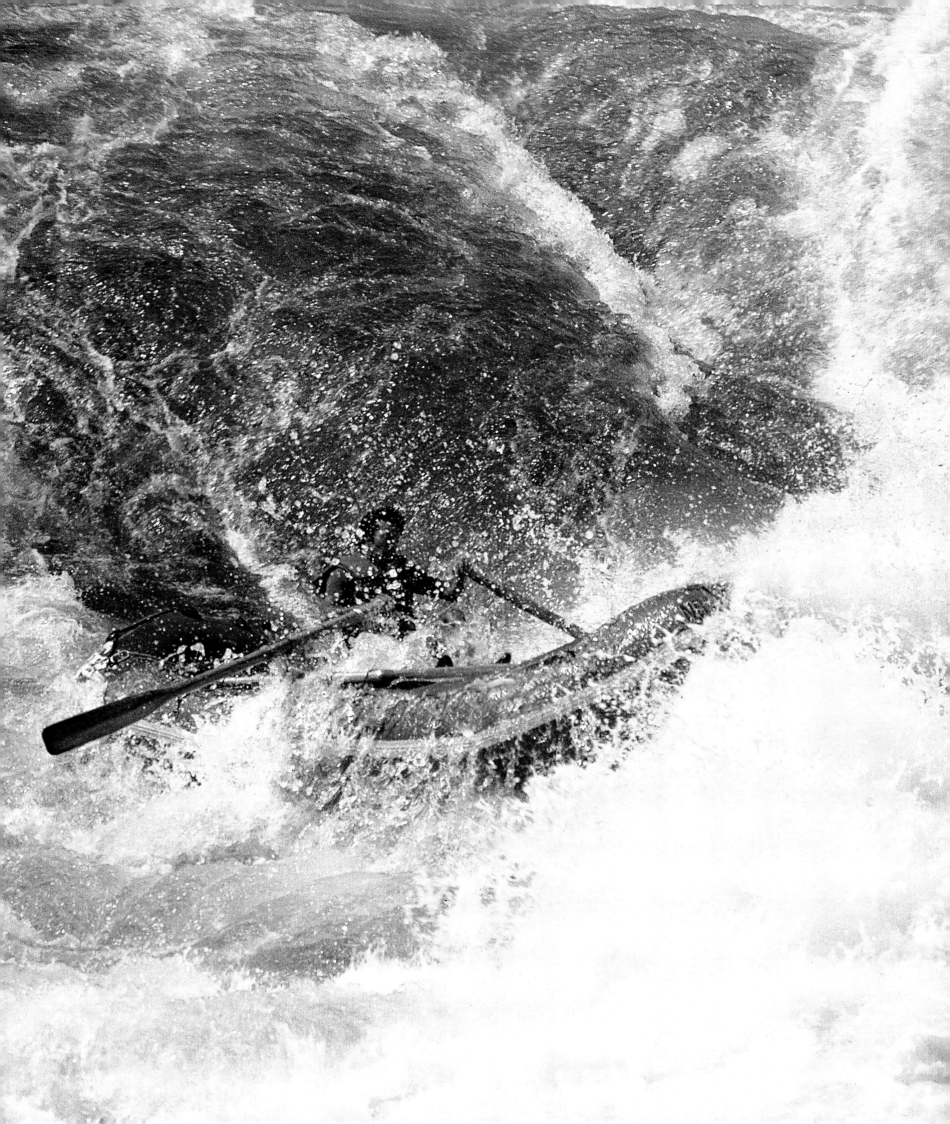

FOREWORD

by Ranulph Fiennes

WHITE WATER: THE WORLD'S WILDEST RIVERS is a book for everyone. The world's whitewater experts will refer to it because it is truly their story, their history. Non-expert dabblers like me, who have merely tasted the thrill and the fear, will shake their heads in awe at what the 'real' water enthusiasts have dared and done. And everyone from children to armchair grandfathers will marvel at the superb photographs of the mind-boggling, daredevil feats attempted and, usually but not always, completed in thundering cataracts all over the world.

The book sensibly starts with a warning that is worth quoting: 'The majority of civilian freshwater drownings take place on flat water, in lakes and pools; moving water merely adds a further dimension to the danger. A person is likely to be rendered unconscious after two minutes underwater without a breath and to suffer death or permanent brain damage within four to twelve minutes thereafter.'

Methods of grading the difficulty and danger of rapids are not of course scientifically exact. Too many factors confuse the issue. But Grade One is described in the book as: 'Fast water with waves but no serious obstructions. Easy. Little danger except for the risks posed by moving water.' At the other extreme – Grade Six – the description reads: 'Extreme water that is continuous and offers no routes of escape. Normally considered unrunnable. Attempted only by extreme risk-takers. A single mistake could be fatal.'

One photograph shows a single kayaker shooting over an abyss with the backdrop of a foaming waterfall. The caption explains that this particular expert on this particular occasion did not make it due to a slight error. His body was never found.

There are photographs of capsized boaters trying to breathe as they are swept down rivers of mud as well as many landscapes of great beauty from remote river valleys all over the world. The author writes movingly of the many ecological threats to these wonderful places and one can but hope that this great and unique book will help at least stem the tide of destruction and pollution posed by loggers, dam construction and other commercial projects worldwide.

If you have ever dipped your toe in white water or even listened in awe to the distant thunder of great falls, you will really enjoy and treasure this book. If you haven't, it may even encourage you to have a go.

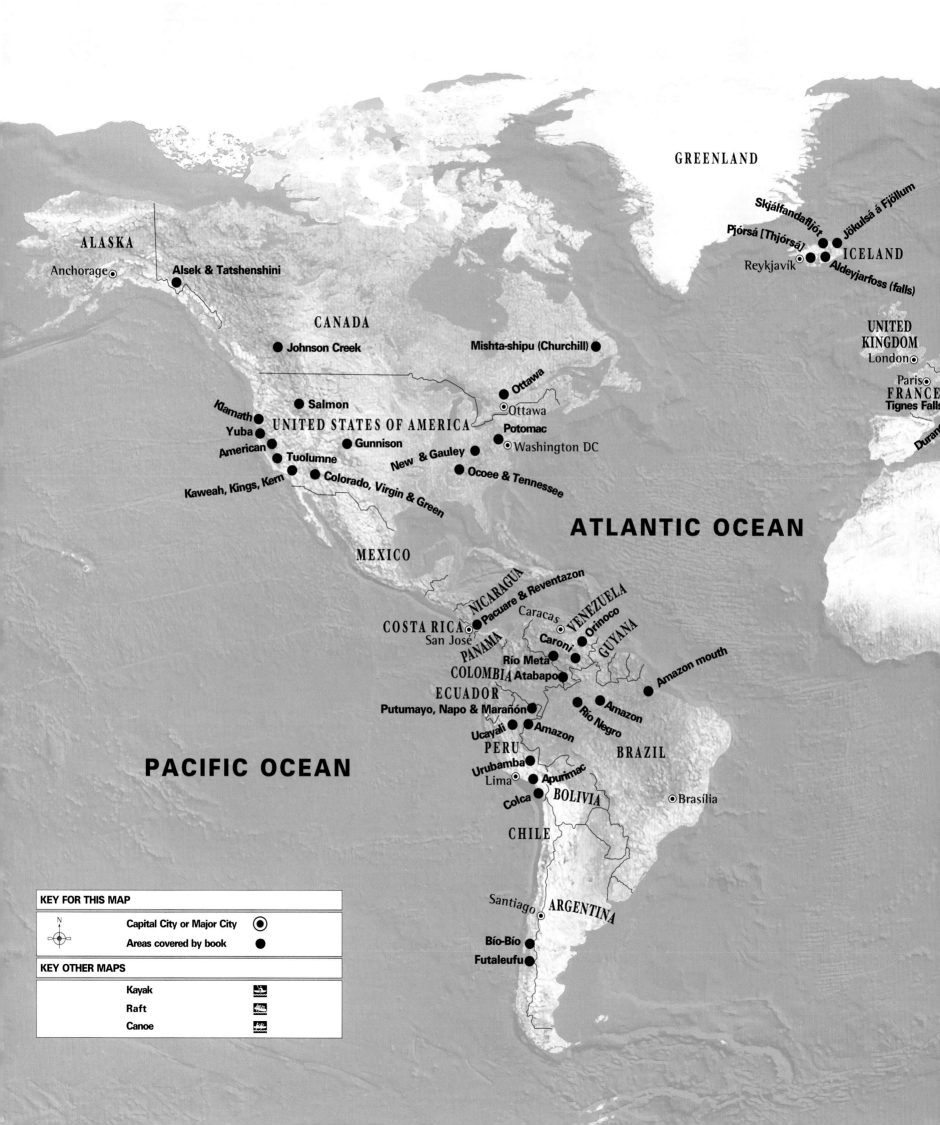

GREENLAND

ALASKA

Anchorage ⊙

Skjálfandafljót

Pjórsá [Thjórsá]   Jökulsá á Fjöllum

Reykjavík ⊙   ICELAND

Aldeyjarfoss (falls)

Alsek & Tatshenshini

UNITED
KINGDOM
London ⊙

CANADA

Johnson Creek

Mishta-shipu (Churchill)

Paris ⊙
FRANCE
Tignes Falls

Ottawa

Klamath   Salmon   ⊙ Ottawa

Yuba   UNITED STATES OF AMERICA   Potomac   Duranc

American   Gunnison   ⊙ Washington DC

Tuolumne

Kaweah, Kings, Kern   Colorado, Virgin & Green   New & Gauley

Ocoee & Tennessee

ATLANTIC OCEAN

MEXICO

NICARAGUA   Pacuare & Reventazon

COSTA RICA   Caracas   VENEZUELA

San José   PANAMA   Caroni   Orinoco   GUYANA

Río Meta

COLOMBIA   Atabapo   Amazon mouth

ECUADOR   Amazon

Putumayo, Napo & Marañón   Río Negro

Ucayali   Amazon   BRAZIL

PACIFIC OCEAN   PERU

Urubamba

Lima ⊙   Apurímac

Colca   BOLIVIA   ⊙ Brasília

CHILE

Santiago ⊙   ARGENTINA

Bío-Bío

Futaleufu

KEY FOR THIS MAP

N

Capital City or Major City   ⊙

Areas covered by book   ●

KEY OTHER MAPS

Kayak

Raft

Canoe

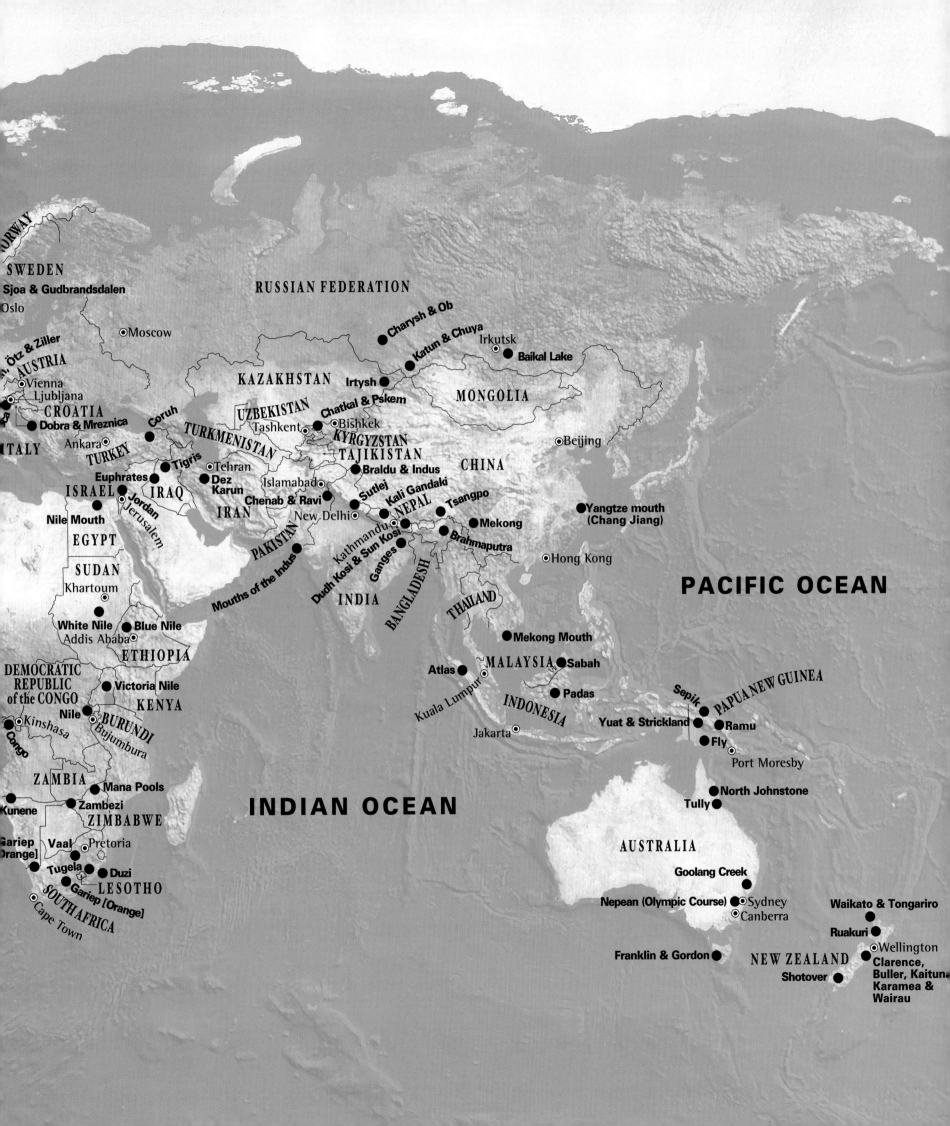

NORWAY

SWEDEN
Sjoa & Gudbrandsdalen
Oslo

RUSSIAN FEDERATION

Moscow

Charysh & Ob

Katun & Chuya Irkutsk

m Ötz & Ziller
AUSTRIA
Vienna
Ljubljana
CROATIA
Dobra & Mreznica **Coruh**
ITALY
Ankara
TURKEY **Tigris**
Euphrates
ISRAEL IRAQ **Dez**
Karun
IRAN

KAZAKHSTAN **Irtysh**

UZBEKISTAN **Chatkal & Pskem**
Tashkent Bishkek
TURKMENISTAN **KYRGYZSTAN**
TAJIKISTAN
Braldu & Indus
Tehran
Islamabad
Chenab & Ravi
New Delhi

MONGOLIA

CHINA

Beijing

Sutlej **Kali Gandaki**
Tsangpo
NEPAL
Mekong
Kathmandu
Brahmaputra
Dudh Kosi & Sun Kosi
Ganges

Yangtze mouth (Chang Jiang)

PAKISTAN

Jordan
Jerusalem

Nile Mouth

EGYPT

SUDAN
Khartoum

Mouths of the Indus

INDIA

Hong Kong

PACIFIC OCEAN

BANGLADESH

THAILAND

White Nile **Blue Nile**
Addis Ababa
ETHIOPIA

Mekong Mouth

Atlas MALAYSIA **Sabah**

DEMOCRATIC
REPUBLIC
of the CONGO
Victoria Nile
KENYA

Sepik PAPUA NEW GUINEA

Kuala Lumpur **Padas**

INDONESIA
Yuat & Strickland **Ramu**

Nile
Kinshasa
BURUNDI
Congo
Bujumbura

Jakarta **Fly**

Port Moresby

ZAMBIA
Mana Pools
Zambezi
ZIMBABWE

INDIAN OCEAN

North Johnstone
Tully

Kunene

Gariep [Orange] **Vaal** Pretoria
Tugela **Duzi**
Gariep [Orange] LESOTHO
SOUTH AFRICA
Cape Town

AUSTRALIA

Goolang Creek

Nepean (Olympic Course) Sydney
Canberra

Waikato & Tongariro
Ruakuri

Franklin & Gordon NEW ZEALAND Wellington
Clarence, Buller, Kaituna Karamea & Wairau
Shotover

ACKNOWLEDGEMENTS

Many personalities with many cracking good stories to tell go into creating a book of this nature. The final interpretations are mine, but without their courage in tackling new rivers and their inputs on river history, expeditions, boat design and paddling technique, this book could never have been written. It needs to be said that there are so many wonderful rivers to choose from that the current selection is to some degree arbitrary – there are just so many pages in a book! My thanks to all who contributed ideas and so helped with the spectacular sampling of whitewater presented here.

In particular I would like to thank those who shared their insights on the challenge of rivers in different countries of the world: Vladimir Gavrilov, Dave Manby, Peter Knowles, Jerome and Morna Truran, Andrew Craven, Peter Winn, Jeffe Aronson, Martin Wong, Bill McGinnis, Eric Hertz, Simon Priest, Steve Nomchong, Zjelko Kelemen, Arlene Burns, Steve Weller, Paul Villecourt, the French guide known only as Runriver, Willem van Riet, Stan Ricketts, Wayne Nicol, Kel Sheppey, Tony Hansen, Sue Liell-Cock, Tony Lightfoot, Allan Ellard, Liam Guilar, Cam McLeay, Stephen Linneweaver, David Allardice, Kieran McKay, Yusuke Fujigaki, and Ruben Gann.

My son Corran Addison, world renowned for his extreme paddling and kayak designs, gained me access to many sources. Various organizations contributed time and resources to the effort: the International Rafting Federation, the Australian and British Canoe Unions, the Southern African Rivers Association and Canoeing SA, and the International Rivers Network. The British Hovercraft Society and the Mad River boating museum helped with specialized historical research. Two sources on ecotourism guided me through the thickets of river politics: Youry B Nemirovksy (tourism around Lake Baikal) and Anu Rao (Innu Nation representative). In addition there were countless Internet sources whose colourful pages often made me want to drop the writing and just go rafting.

Finally, the text passed through the hands of two patient and dedicated editors, Lauren Copley and Mariëlle Renssen, and was expertly managed by Claudia dos Santos and Lois O'Brien. I thank them all. My wife Karen and adopted son Damian loyally took holidays and weekends alone while I paddled my computer.

SAFETY ON RIVERS AND THE GRADING OF RAPIDS

Caution: Readers of this book are strongly advised not to attempt whitewater boating without the proper guidance, even for relatively 'safe' rivers. The majority of civilian freshwater drownings take place on flat water, in lakes and pools; moving water merely adds a further dimension to the danger. A person is likely to be rendered unconscious after two minutes underwater without a breath, and to suffer death or permanent brain damage within four to 12 minutes thereafter, depending on one's physiology and the water temperature.

It is especially important to realize that many of the rivers featured here are mostly of higher grade and are at the limits of what is considered runnable even by experts. Grade 4, 5 and 6 river-running are simply not for everybody. The pressure of friends to compete, one's own eagerness, and the persuasiveness of some operators should not blind one to the real, and potentially fatal, risks of entering the river's cauldron. Keep in mind that good leadership is a prerequisite for safe boating. Good leaders are those who have done 'river time' over many years. They come properly equipped for the river in question and are qualified to carry out swiftwater rescue and emergency procedures. They show an empathy with others who may not be as confident or strong as they are. Never be afraid to ask about the background of river guides, or to press them for answers to questions about trip organization and precautions.

GRADING

No truly objective method of grading or classing the difficulty and danger of rapids exists. Too many factors enter the picture, though as a rule of thumb the international 1–6 grading system does give some idea of what to expect (and what to avoid). Rivers change daily and seasonally, river boats perform differently, and boaters vary greatly in skill and experience. Risks increase if the water is extremely cold or the weather closes in, while the consequences of an accident worsen if the party is in a remote area. Difficulty may be accentuated by the state of mind of the party, especially if they are exhausted. Although the river's flow regime (volume and gradient) is measurable, experience on rivers counts more than any other factor when assessing a run.

Most experienced river-runners use the 'six difficulty classes' enumerated by American Whitewater, a non-profit association representing paddlers and promoting whitewater sport. First adopted in 1959 and revised in 1998, the code is at www.awa.org/awa/safety/safety.html It is replete with advice on personal and group equipment and preparedness.

Note: The following are common international rapid grading guidelines adapted by the author to distinguish difficulty and danger.

GRADE/CLASS	DESCRIPTION	DIFFICULTY	DANGER
1 or I	Fast water with waves but no serious obstructions.	Easy.	Little danger except for the risks posed by moving water.
2 or II	Rapid that requires some manoeuvring.	Easy, but it may challenge the inexperienced.	Somewhat risky if people hit rocks or take swims.
3 or III	Big, noisy and complex, with rocks, currents and turns.	Not very easy, requires nerve and co-ordination. Possible for crews with good skippers.	Moderate danger, especially from long swims or pinnings on rocks.
4 or IV	Wild and powerful water which can be scouted to plan the route, but surprises are likely.	Difficult – beyond the competence of the average touring boater.	Dangerous to swimmers, and likely to wrap rafts on rocks.
5 or V	Long, violent, unpredictable rapid with multiple channels, drops, holes, and surges. Poor visibility makes scouting very risky.	Only experts should attempt this type of rapid.	Extremely dangerous – injuries and drowning are real possibilities.
6 or VI	Extreme water that is continuous and offers no routes of escape.	Normally considered unrunnable. Attempted only by extreme risk-takers.	A single mistake could be fatal.

INTRODUCTION

THE INEXORABLE PULL OF WHITEWATER

World civilization was born on the great rivers: the Nile of Ancient Egypt, the Euphrates-Tigris in Mesopotamia, the Yangtze in China, the Niger in Benin, and the upper Amazon in the Andes. Many great rivers start life as torrents springing cold and green from the foot of glaciers, seeping from mountain tarns, or bursting brown and noisy from the depths of cloud forests drenched by the seasonal monsoon. They accelerate and grow to mighty waterways.

The world's great whitewater rivers are today at the frontiers of true adventure. As this is written, discoverers are carrying out first descents on rivers hidden in the deepest folds of the Himalayas and the remotest parts of Siberia. Braving warfare, they are riding the rapids in Central Africa's Mountains of the Moon and, despite the presence of terrorists and armed bands of drug-runners, tackling the upper tributaries of South America's Amazon River in Peru and Ecuador. The pioneers use small boats that seem puny by comparison with the forces of the river. Yet their canoes, hard-hulled dories, kayaks, inflatable rafts — and lately even riverboards barely big enough to float the torso — have taken them where no fur trappers or military expeditions ever could go or dared to venture.

Rivers are pervasive, even in deserts like the infinitely bleak Namib in Southern Africa, where dry watercourses erupt with molten chocolate flash floods after rainfall. The world's oldest desert, the Namib is a region of shifting sand dunes and emaciated rocky hills ridging like ocean waves to the horizon. The plateau landscape is gashed with startling abruptness by a 550m (1800ft) canyon, surpassed in barren grandeur only by the Grand Canyon of the Colorado River in the USA; but the difference is that the Namib's Fish River rarely flows. When it does, the kayakers and rafters appear. Their whoops of delight echo from the walls, blending with the rumble of rocks being rolled along the bottom by the extraordinary force of the current.

Wild rivers beckon us with their power and the majesty of their scenery. They stir the adrenaline in the blood, and the rhythms of their moving waters pulse through us like our own heartbeats.

ABOVE, LEFT TO RIGHT: *The little-known Fish River canyon in the Namib Desert of Southern Africa; the well-known Grand Canyon of the Colorado River in Arizona; the Rhondu Gorges on the Indus River in Pakistan, with kayaks awaiting more action.*
RIGHT: *A raft heads into a mass of white water on the Colorado River, Grand Canyon. The oarsman is facing forwards, in the classic portegee position.*

The past few decades have brought a remarkable increase in the numbers of ordinary people running rivers for thrills and relaxation. An element of fear usually forms part of the adventure travel mix. Given our historic association with rivers, it is not too strange that we tend to seek excitement on high mountain cataracts, following rivers wherever they may lead. 'Messing about in boats' includes deliberately courting danger and testing one's nerve against the churning currents in secret valleys and rock-strewn gorges.

The rivers that we think of as constituents of national identity, like the Mississippi, the Volga, the Murray/Darling, the Seine and the Thames, are companions of our tired industrial lifestyles — polluted, busy, hemmed

ABOVE: *A modern crew runs the Grand Canyon with the original type of oarboat, equipment and clothing used by John Wesley Powell on his first trip down the Grand Canyon in 1859. This sequence is a commemorative recreation of events by* National Geographic *magazine.*

OPPOSITE: *Traditional reed boat, known as a tankwa, pictured beside Lake Tana in Ethiopia.*

THE DEVELOPMENT OF WHITEWATER RIVER BOATING

1842
American inventor Horace Day builds first inflatable rubber raft and patents it in 1846.
John Fremont uses 'air army boat' to survey Platte River, Nebraska, USA.

1848
US Naval expedition under Lieut William Lynch descends Jordan River, Israel, to Dead Sea.

1850s
Loggers run rapids on South Fork of American River in bateaux, light simple boats made from large boards.

1855
Dr David Livingstone travels down Zambezi River by canoe and is the first European to see Musi-oa-Tunya, which he names Victoria Falls.

1855
Mark Twain's novel, *Huckleberry Finn*, describes a houseboat raft that floats down the Mississippi River, USA.

1858
John Hanning Speke believes he has found source of Nile at Mwanza, in south of Lake Victoria, East Africa.

1866
Scotsman John MacGregor builds first of five versions of kayak, *Rob Roy*. He founds Royal Canoe Club.

1867
Wild West horse thief James White claims to be first person to run Grand Canyon, on a floating log.

1869
American John Wesley Powell leads an expedition on first descent of Grand Canyon in wooden boats. Powell is regarded by many as the true father of whitewater boating. He again ran the canyon in 1871.

THE DEVELOPMENT OF WHITEWATER BOATS

The origins of whitewater boats are lost in time, as are the tales of the first journeys by moving water. Fishermen manoeuvre dugouts with great skill on rivers in Central Africa to set and retrieve fish-capture baskets and nets strung across rapids.

As long as 7000 years ago, inflatable rafts were used on the Euphrates and Tigris in Mesopotamia. The use of the kalak, a timber raft supported on inflated goatskins, remains very widespread in Asia. In the 19th century, Prussian military strategist Count Helmuth von Moltke was conveyed by skin raft during a trip on the Euphrates. The modern Russian ploht raft, seen at river festivals in Siberia, is similar: a platform supported by rubber tubes.

Technologies of boating have spread across the continents and may also have helped peoples to cross the oceans. A large balsa raft of a type common in South America was sailed by the Swedish explorer Thor Heyerdahl, when he crossed the Pacific on the Kon-Tiki in 1947. The raft drifted from Peru, South America, to near Tahiti, providing evidence for a theory of trans-Pacific migration. Heyerdahl also navigated across from Africa to South America in an Egyptian papyrus raft. Traditional reed rafts are still used on the Nile and, known as caballitos, are paddled by fishermen in Peru.

Native North Americans developed the tree bark canoe, sewing the skin of the birch together around a flexible wooden frame and sealing it with pine resin. Around AD1000 these Indian canoes were observed by the son of Eric the Red, Leif Ericsson, during his extended trip from Greenland to Newfoundland and probably to New England. In the 18th century, the French-Canadian voyageurs adopted the birch bark design for large canoes in which they conveyed pelts and furs down-river to coastal ports.

Kayaks, sea-going craft used for hunting, originated with the Eskimos of Greenland and spread to Alaska. In the mid-1700s, David Crantz, a missionary in Greenland, listed 10 methods of Eskimo-rolling a kayak. The kayak transferred comfortably to rivers in the 19th century, and today the skill of rolling is basic to successful whitewater kayaking.

The river dory is an open rowing boat with sealed buoyancy chambers, providing a smooth and exciting ride through big water. The master of dory design and handcrafting was American riverman Martin Litton who in his late seventies was still regularly rowing a dory down the Grand Canyon of the Colorado.

1869
Scot John MacGregor descends upper Jordan River near Lake Galilee, Israel.

1876
Henry Morton Stanley follows Lualaba and Congo rivers from Lake Tanganyika (Great Rift Valley) to Atlantic Ocean.

1890
Tatshenshini River, Canada, run in a dugout canoe by English explorer Edward James Glave, Great North West pioneer Jack Dalton and two Tlingit Indians.

1896
Nathaniel Galloway revolutionizes whitewater oar boating by turning his seat around to face downstream.

1907
Folding kayak patented by German Johannes Klepper, initiating worldwide exploration of rivers.

1909
USA's first paid whitewater trip led by Julius Stone, who runs Grand Canyon using Nathaniel Galloway's technique.

1920s
US Army develops life rafts for aeroplanes.

1920s–30s
In USA and Canada, river-running becomes a recreational sport, using dories and scows.

1937
The O-ring, essential for the waterproofing of containers, is patented by Niels Christensen; in 1941 it is licensed to United Aircraft. Rubber ring in slot takes four years of testing to perfect as hydraulic system seal.

RIGHT: *Fishermen on the Indus River in Pakistan stand atop the earliest form of inflatable raft: a platform resting on blown-up animal skins.*
OPPOSITE: *North rim, Grand Canyon, Arizona.*

in by roads and construction works, carriers of coal barges and casino paddle steamers. The greatest river of all, the Amazon, sprawls across a steamy basin in a channel so broad, dolphins swim right up it, considering it to be a kind of sea. Higher up, it is fraught with danger as it claws at the heart of the Andes, cutting canyons so narrow and vertical that in some places boaters are in constant peril from plummeting rocks. The rivergods are fickle, and no respecters of persons.

The world's great whitewater rivers are symbols of all that is wild and free. In the past century they have been dammed and destroyed at an alarming rate, but still they appeal to something in the human spirit that is forever yearning for the thrill of a physical challenge and the pleasures of solitude.

Wild rivers are the ruffians of the planet. They rebel against order. Darkened by storms, a flooding river rips through farmlands and towns, plundering the earth of its soil and destroying life as much as, in calmer days, it nurtures it. For the river guides who live and work on rivers, or those that join them for the experience, the mystique and turmoil of the river represents something that has vanished from the comfort zones of civilization.

THE MODERN AGE OF RIVER EXPLORATION

Every generation since time began has had its own way of expressing humanity's bond with the world's great rivers. Rivers have always been used for trade, sometimes for military conquest, and usually as barriers between peoples,

marking national boundaries. Starting in the 1860s, however, rivers became recreational destinations, routes to adventure with no particular purpose but the thrill of exploration and self-actualization through meeting the challenge of nature. By the 1950s, river-running was well established amongst a small, hard-bitten coterie of boaters in Europe and North America. Then came the boom in popular participation, as the post-war generation bought up US army surplus inflatables and began the rush to raft rivers that has persisted to this day.

The Baby Boomers pioneered many new routes; they were followed by Generation X who turned rivers into rodeo boating playgrounds; and now the daredevils of the Millennium generation are pushing the limits, running more and more extreme cataracts and waterfalls –

while the bulk of ordinary river-runners continue to raft for fun. Yet they are the beneficiaries of developments at the cutting edge, like the average motorist whose car is equipped with microchip technology derived from spacecraft. Paddlers of all kinds rely on equipment and skills spurred by river exploration at the ends of the earth.

Technology, the rise of river guiding, and the accessibility of rivers in the USA and Europe allowed the rafting craze to take off. In recent decades it has spread to other continents and far less accessible rivers. New Zealanders and Australians, South Americans, Russians and South Africans have all advanced the discipline of river-running by studying the dynamics of moving water and fearlessly tackling unknown watercourses. Materials for river boats in all climates and conditions have also evolved. Despite

1938
Americans pioneer their home rivers: Amos Burg runs Middle Fork of Salmon River in an inflatable raft. First commercial trips by Norman Nevills down Grand Canyon, USA.

1939
American John D Whiting and three companions paddle Jordan (Israel) in folding (Klepper) kayaks.

1940
Fisherman designs McKenzie drift boat to float rivers and plunge over waves in heavy water.

1942
First folding boat descent of the Salmon River, Idaho, USA. First recreational descent in scow, followed later by rowboats and dories.

1945–1950s
Grumman Aircraft work with aluminium stockpiles left over from World War II to build famous Grumman Canoe.

1950s–70s
Canoe and folding boat racing becomes very popular in USA.

1952
American Bus Hatch granted first concession to take paying customers down Grand Canyon, USA.

1953
South African Ian Player launches tough canoe marathon on Umsindusi River, KwaZulu-Natal, South Africa.

American John M Goddard and two companions kayak Nile from its highest source to the sea, missing big rapids. Remotest headstream is the Ruvyironza River of Burundi.

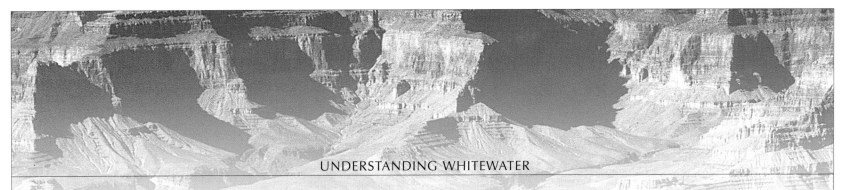

UNDERSTANDING WHITEWATER

Many people think of the shape of a river as a series of curving S-bends leading to the sea, which is not an accurate picture. This meandering form is typical only of the lower course or trunk of a river – what hydrologists call its mature stage as it slows down on the final stage of its journey.

A river is shaped like a tree, with its branches in the mountains, its trunk forming the main watercourse, and its roots in the estuary or delta. The river-tree grows upwards and outwards as tributaries cut back into higher ground. The trunk is the main channel carrying what is called the transport load (eroded silt, floating debris and pollutants like sewage). The fan-like delta system spreads outwards into the ocean as the river deposits sediment at its mouth.

The ancient Chinese philosopher Lao-tzu once said that water represented 'the highest excellence'. He was referring to water's tendency to run to the lowest spot and remain still, without a desire to go anywhere else. River-runners turn Lao-tzu on his head; for them, the highest kind of excellence is the restless motion of the water.

Rapids, or whitewater, can occur at almost any stage of a river's progress as it descends. In the mountains, continuous staircase rapids or cataracts come tumbling down over the boulders, forming steep chutes with tight eddies. Boating here involves quick decision-making and much bouncing over ledges, with the constant danger that a waterfall may lie just around the next bend.

In its middle course, a river may seem to slow down but there is evidence that the current in midstream is a lot faster than it was in the mountains. Dykes of hard rock form rapids by damming back the current, which then surges over the drops. Deep hollows develop where the softer rock is eroded or faulted, thus creating what is known as pool-and-drop rapids.

High waterfalls are a feature of the mountainous upper courses of rivers that nowadays attract daredevils to run them in kayaks and small inflatables. Wide major falls like Niagara between Canada/USA and the Victoria Falls between Zimbabwe/Zambia occur in the middle course of rivers at geological faults and escarpments.

As the river approaches its end, a narrowing of the channel or a sudden bend may create enormous turbulence as the current is crammed into less space and forced to speed up. Another source of turbulence at every stage of the river's course from the mountains to the lowlands is the confluence of two currents in the same river or two rivers. The waters collide in boils and whirls.

A hole, or 'hydraulic', occurs when the current pours over a rock and backs on itself: this area of suck-back is normally marked by a foaming pile of water with aerated boils erupting downstream of it. Bad holes are known as 'keepers' and those from which there may be no escape can be killers. The worst of them are often the man-made low-head dams or weirs over which the flow is wide and sheer. Boats and swimmers may be trapped in the slot below the weir with no way to break free unless they are thrown a rescue line or they get 'flushed out' by the bottom current. For those who like to test their paddling skills against the forces of the river, holes with big foam piles are river rodeo – or freestyle playboating – arenas.

Given the river's geological profile – its hard granites and soft lavas, its cliffs and sandbanks – rapids are large or small depending on steepness and flow.

As a basis for comparison, the Orinoco River in the Amazon Basin is a gigantic flood of water in a normal rainy season, hitting 42,000 cumecs, or 1.5 million cfs. The Colorado River in the Grand Canyon, regarded as a 'big Western river' by North American standards, has a fairly good flow when 340 cumecs, or 12,000 cfs, is released from the Glen Canyon dam – the Orinoco is equal to 125 Colorados! But the difference in gradient is perhaps more telling. The Orinoco, though extremely wild in some sections, is flat for much of its course, while the Colorado has hundreds of rapids dispersed along its length and is deservedly seen as a great whitewater river.

1955
Hovercraft patented by British engineer Christopher Cockerell.

1956
Section of Indus River rafted for first time to make film for broadcaster Lowell Thomas.

1960s
Hard-hulled kayaks and dories become fun-boats for river-running. Fibreglass kayaks and canoes emerge from Europe; first custom-designed dories built by American Martin Litton.

First wetsuits and lightweight, comfortable, personal flotation devices (PFDs) manufactured.

Czechs visit USA and impart new enthusiasm for precision paddling and racing.

1961
Two American students kayak Alsek River, Alaska, bypassing Turnback Canyon.

1965
Kunene River, Angola, paddled by South Africans Willem van Riet and Gordon Rowe.

American Bryce Whitmore lashes pontoons together with rowing frames to make rafts requiring no bailing.

1968
US Wild and Scenic Rivers System enacted by Congress to protect designated rivers.

Briton John Blashford-Snell leads UK expedition partway down Blue Nile in Ethiopia.

1969
River catches fire: Cuyahoga River in industrial Cleveland, Ohio, USA, burns with pollutants.

LEFT: *A kayaker flies over a drop on the Gunnison River. The river cuts a steep-sided gorge 520m (1700ft) deep, and 396m (1300ft) at its widest.*

its prominence, the so-called rubber raft is not solely, or even primarily, responsible for creating the modern sport of river-running. Exploration has depended in large part on the development of four types of river craft: flat-bottomed boats such as the cumbersome wooden scow and later the dory rowboat; the open canoe, usually of aluminium or durable plastic; the inflatable raft made of rubberized fabric, hypalon or PVC; and the kayak fashioned from hard-shell fibreglass or pliable plastics to fend off rocks.

After World War II, a flood of military surplus rafts and lightweight canoes hit the American market, enabling back-country explorers to run local rivers over weekends and try longer journeys as their grasp of the sport grew. By the mid-1970s, kayaks — craft originally used by the Inuit (Eskimo) peoples for hunting at sea — had emerged as versatile river boats capable of highly technical manoeuvres. If the raft was mass-marketed as a kind of rubber bucking bronco for big whitewater, by the 1990s the kayak was king of the mountain creeks. Through it all, dory boaters finessed the rapids in their graceful craft, and wilderness-loving canoeists continued to push into the wild backwaters far from roads and help.

Exploration trips down unknown rivers are very costly, requiring sponsorships and thus media publicity which in turn fuels further public curiosity. The foremost American river explorer of his day, Richard Bangs, has run numerous river expeditions in America, Asia, Africa and the Far East. He and fellow American John Yost started the Sobek company (named after the crocodile god of

---

1970s
Rafting starts to catch on in Europe, with trips in Alps and Pyrenees. Russian rafters begin to explore rivers in the Pamirs and establish a route on Bashkaus River in Sayan mountains of Siberia.

1971
Sun Kosi River, Nepal, paddled, then rafted. Artificial river rapids built for Olympics at Augsburg, Bavaria.

American Walt Blackadar washed down Turnback Canyon on Alsek River, Alaska, and survives.

1972
Frenchman Michel Peissel's hovercraft penetrates Himalayas up Kali Gandaki River to Tibet.

Blue Nile gorges paddled by British kayakers under Mike Jones.

1973
Plastic kayak developed and tested on rocky section of Kern River, California, USA.

Richard Bangs and pioneers of Sobek begin explorations with trip down Omo River, Ethiopia.

Tugela River gorge in Zululand, KwaZulu-Natal, South Africa, is kayaked.

1974
Czech team runs part of Dudh Kosi, Nepal.

1975
First formal river rodeo at Stanley, on Salmon River, Idaho, USA.

Utah University professor and kayaker J Calvin Giddings and friends run Apurimac River, Peru, South America.

THE POPULARIZING OF WHITEWATER THROUGH MOVIES

Deliverance Rock juts into the bustling Chattooga River like a grey, ugly building. The river, cascading through misty conifer forests in the Appalachians bordering on Georgia and South Carolina in southeastern USA, culminates in famous rapids such as the Five Falls and Soc'em Dog. Here the film Deliverance was made. Written by novelist James Dickey and directed with brooding imagination by John Boorman, it is the story of four Atlanta business friends on a canoe trip that goes disastrously wrong.

Two mountain men walk out of the forest and at shotgun-point sodomize Bobby, one of the businessmen. Actor Burt Reynolds, playing the part of Lewis, kills a hillbilly with a bow and arrow, whereupon the canoeists make their escape down the gorge – only to be hunted by the other mountain man with the shotgun. Lewis breaks his leg when his canoe capsizes, and leaving him at Deliverance Rock, his friend Ed, played by Jon Voight, climbs the cliff to finish off the hillbilly once and for all with another arrow.

Somehow, you can never float past the rock without looking hard to see if Burt Reynolds is still lying on that ledge writhing in agony. The film was first screened as long ago as 1972, but this tale of violence and escape remains very much a part of the lore of rivers today. More than any other media event of its time, it promoted the recreational river-running craze that was taking off in the USA and spreading across the globe.

Perhaps rivers offer a gruelling test of bravery in a society that no longer recognizes the raw forces of the wilderness. Rivers flow beyond the borders of civilized life; the official rules that regulate our lives are suspended and human nature must confront the brutal natural world. Running the river is a form of initiation into manhood.

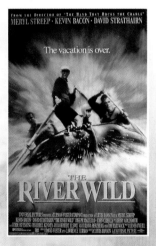

Two decades after Deliverance, actress Meryl Streep played the role of a female river guide in The River Wild, *a thrilling, if predictable, portrayal of rafting on the Kootenai River in northern Montana, USA. In the intervening years, much had changed in the general attitude towards rivers and those who took them on. Streep played the role of a demoralized housewife and mother escaping back into the valley where she had grown up and once worked as a pro rafter. A couple of robbers accost the party and Streep emerges as the heroine after successfully piloting her craft through the 'The Gauntlet' (actually, the Kootenai Falls) while her husband and son look to her for leadership. In this movie, once again, the elements of gangsterism, extreme fear and unchecked nature come together in the rapids in a symbolic re-enactment of river myth, but this time the river is no longer an arena for the display of muscles and male courage; the central figure is a woman with family values.*

The Kootenai Indians, inhabitants since the 1500s of the glacial valley where the translucent river crashes over the falls, regard the area as sacred and believe that it is a place for visions and meditation. Early white pioneers were frankly frightened by the thundering falls which drop a total of some 91m (300ft) over a short distance. To film the raft sequences in The River Wild *in 1993, Universal Studios first had to get the permission of the tribe, and then used dummies over the falls.*

Kootenai is the last major waterfall on a northwestern USA river not yet harnessed for hydro power. Nowadays extreme kayakers delightedly shoot sections of the Kootenai Falls, happy in the knowledge that successive attempts to dam the falls have all failed to materialize.

1976
British team under Mike Jones does partial descent of Dudh Kosi, Nepal.

Rob Lesser and other young adventurers join Walt Blackadar on Alaska's Susitna River.

1977
Rob Lesser runs Devil's Canyon, Susitna River, dubbed 'Everest' of whitewater.

Sobek establishes runs on various high-grade rivers in New Guinea.

Apurimac and Urubamba rivers in Peru are rafted by Westerners.

1978
Sobek completes descent of Bío-Bío River, Chile.

Walt Blackadar drowns on South Fork of Payette River, Idaho, USA. Mike Jones is drowned on Braldu River, Pakistan.

1979
Hell's Gate on Fraser River, British Columbia, Canada, is rafted.

Sobek runs parts of Indus River below Skardu and Gilgit in Kashmir.

Rafters chain themselves to rocks to protest damming of Stanislaus River, California, USA.

1981
Australian team led by John Wilde runs the Sun Kosi River, Nepal.

1980s–1990s
Kayak designers develop lower-volume, shorter boats for general playing and squirt-boating.

1980s
Self-bailing inflatable rafts developed; widely adopted.

First descents of serious Grade 4–5 rivers by 'joy boys' of kayaking in the USA.

1980s
Numerous Himalayan rivers finally kayaked or rafted; commercial operations begin.

Guided river trips become established in Australia, New Zealand, Southern Africa, Central and South America.

1981
Commercial rafting on Grade 4–5 sections of Tuolumne River, California, gets under way.

Sobek rafts Batoka Gorge of Zambezi River.

1985–86
Yangtze River, China, paddled by competing Chinese and American groups; two groups go source to sea.

1986
Holme Pierrepont whitewater sports centre opened in Nottingham, England (slalom canoeing and rafting).

1987
French paddler François Ciroteau establishes world waterfall record with descent of two-tier 28m (92ft) fall in Pyrenees.

Americans Arlene Burns and Dan Dixon paddle upper Tsangpo River, Tibet.

1988
Rapids '-1' and '-2' below Victoria Falls kayaked.

1989
South African Corran Addison kayaks over Tignes

Falls on Isere River, French Alps, establishing unofficial world record of 31m (101.68ft).

Australia's North Johnstone River, near Cairns, gets World Heritage status; kayakers begin to explore it.

Luapula River, major tributary of Congo, kayaked by South Africans Tony Hansen and Phil Lloyd.

International paddlers join Chuya River rally in Russia under aegis of Project Raft. An international sub-culture of river-running develops between former Cold War enemies.

1990
British team paddles Rhondu gorges of Indus River in Pakistan.

1990s
During this decade, extreme kayakers run many remote mountain and jungle rivers, from Quijos, Ecuador, to Pungwe, Zimbabwe.

1991
Jan Kellner from Germany becomes first world kayak rodeo (freestyle) champion. Freestyle kayaking takes off as a new spectator sport.

1994
First descent of upper Mekong River, China, by American Peter Winn.

1996
Leading up to 1996, artificial rapids shaped in bed of Ocoee River, Tennessee, for 1996 Olympics.

Rapids of Victoria Nile below Bujagali Falls, Uganda, rafted by New Zealander Cam McLeay and team.

Richard Bangs and group of 21 float down the 2130m-deep (7000ft) Tekeze canyon, Ethiopia.

Ancient Egypt) to fund their obsession, offering catered trips for risk-prone paying adventure travellers whom they persuaded to accompany them to outlandish places like Ethiopia and Zimbabwe. Bangs has been a role model for many modern-day wilderness leaders; for like other 'river rats', he is content when he hears the boom of unscouted rapids ahead and senses a story of danger and the spirit of adventure hanging in the humid air.

There are no imitators in this game, only those who learn by doing. Out there on the river, every seasoned boater you meet is a character, drawing something rebellious and fatalistic from the lifeblood of the river gods.

SAFETY AND SURVIVAL IN WHITEWATER

Whitewater rafting is the leading form of 'hard' adventure in the world today. Statistically, rafting was found to be the most popular high-risk adventure sport in a 1997 survey done by the Travel Industry Association of America. Nevertheless, it takes courage to participate, which is why whitewater rafting is classed as a hard adventure. Although its adherents are vastly outnumbered by 'soft' adventurers who prefer fishing and hiking, river-running is for those who take their thrills seriously.

Nothing in this book should suggest to the reader that river-running is always easy or safe. Rafting has been described as the aquatic equivalent of skydiving out of an aeroplane when you could touch down safely instead. Many of the trips described here were executed by advanced/expert boaters, while lesser skilled novices would have been foolhardy to go along for the ride. An accident can happen at any moment; even experts do drown. Leading British kayaker Mike Jones perished on the Braldu River in Pakistan in 1978 on a day when the party was merely warming up for a trip to come. He was washed into a severely undercut cliff-face and his body was never found.

Boating is not like climbing a mountain – mountains are immovable, but a river is in constant process, carrying the paddler from situation to situation. Moving water is pocked with hazards, ranging from fanged rocks to vicious recirculating holes. A person who has once swum a serious rapid will know that the briefest glimpse, snatched as you ride over the crest of a wave, can provide the vital information needed for taking evasive action and swimming determinedly for safety.

Most of the dynamics in the water cannot be seen because they occur deeper in the body of the flow, and can only be 'read' or inferred by the boater looking at the surface. Much depends on aptitudes developed by time on the river, by one's feel for the water, since the laws of fluid dynamics are so complex they have never yet been modelled by even the most sophisticated computers. Experience is everything.

Claims of 'first descents' in river-running are difficult to substantiate, so in general the explorers featured here are given credit for their pioneering efforts without necessarily saying they were the first to run a particular river. And for ourselves, in going down these rivers we may still experience the same excitement as when they were run for the first time. No matter how often a river is boated, or how well we get to know its every mood, every run is a fresh challenge and the river can dish up surprises.

There are many rivers to run, many gullys erupting with floodwater, rainforest rivers unknown, chill Arctic streams, crashing between iced banks and rising to the summer warmth. The threat and the test are there, awaiting collectors of river wisdom.

Previous Pages: *Rafters on the Tamur River, Nepal, head into a wild channel broken by boulders.*
Right: *Paddlers become airborne as their raft drops into a slot on the Marsyandi River, Nepal.*

1996
Joint USA-China expedition completes several legs of Nujiang, or Salween, River to promote ecotourism; government insists on scientific and social aims.

1997
Nepal's last unrun big river, Thule Bheri, paddled by American kayakers, including Scott Lindgren.

1998
World waterfall record set by 20-year-old woman kayaker, Shannon Carroll, on 23.7m (78ft) Sahalie Falls, McKenzie River, Oregon.

1999
Steve Fisher of South Africa takes world record for highest freewheel over 12.2m (40ft) fall in Oregon. Nico Chassing of France takes new world freewheel title over a 16.7m (55ft) fall, also in Oregon.

1999–2000
Artificial rapids built and used at Penrith, near Sydney, for the Millennium Olympic Games.

2000
Black American team uses hydrospeeds for descent of Trisuli River, Himalayas.

NORTH AMERICA

TATSHENSHINI & ALSEK * SALMON * AMERICAN * COLORADO * OCOEE * NEW

The rapids of North America are legendary around every campfire where rivers are discussed and their merits touted. Although modern Americans did not invent river recreation, they have certainly done a lot to perfect it, aided by wide public appreciation and abetted by government backing in the form of legislation to protect scenic rivers. The USA alone has over 5.6 million kilometres (3.5 million miles) of rivers and streams nourishing farms and cities, sustaining wildlife and satisfying the craving of millions for 'splash' action.

It is somewhat surprising that this largely flat continent has so many steep waterways. Its average elevation is a mere 720m (2360ft), compared with that of the highest (but driest) continent, Antarctica, with an elevation of 2300m (7544ft). But America's abundant rain and snowfall, flushing off the sides of the Rocky Mountains in the west and the Appalachians in the east, have carved mighty river gorges and laid down vast flood plains on the landscape. From 18,000 years ago, glaciers began to retreat across the great Canadian Shield — a broad, stable plateau of ancient Precambrian rocks in northern Canada, stretching from Labrador on the east coast to Mackenzie Basin on the west and up to the Arctic. Uncountable lakes were left behind. Fresh water, standing or flowing, is thus the greatest adventure travel resource of the North American continent.

As a result, Americans have always been river-runners. A long heritage of hunting and trapping by canoe has translated, today, into the gritty familiarity with rivers by which professional river guides in their thousands ply their trade. The guides, muscled and bronzed, friendly, a bit whacky in their attitudes and habits, are emblematic of a classic rafting culture that has multiplied into an international phenomenon. Virtually every regional set of rivers has a detailed guidebook. Persistent media coverage has reinforced the love of all things wild and watery. There are so many operators (called 'outfitters') that on some weekends in midsummer the more popular rivers can look like multi-lane highways for 'rubber buses' (rafts). But much-prized solitude is still possible for the average boater as there are so many runnable rivers. Extremists are pushing further and further into the remote canyons of the Rockies, Appalachians and other ranges. Adventurers in canoes, kayaks and rafts are crossing the vast glaciated plains of lakeland Canada and discovering the steamy, wild rivers of Mexico.

ABOVE LEFT: *The Tuolumne River flows through a wilderness canyon near Yosemite National Park, California.*
ABOVE CENTRE: *Massive abutments of rock and desert cliffs loom over the Colorado River in the Grand Canyon.*
ABOVE RIGHT: *The Tatshenshini/Alsek River sweeps out of British Columbia into the Glacier Bay National Preserve of Alaska.*
OPPOSITE: *Colorado River rapids explode with dramatic force as the river carries wild, churning mudwater after heavy rain.*

CANADA AND ALASKA

Canada and Alaska are regions that have a rich river inheritance. White ribbons erupt from the ice to cascade through seemingly endless deep green fir forests; glaciers weep everlasting streams into the bleak tundra; and lakes, ponds and bogs seep multitudes of brooks that combine to make formidable rivers.

The first great Westerner to explore Canada, the Frenchman Jacques Cartier, used rivers in his attempt to cross America in search of the East. In 1535 two Indian youths told Cartier about routes across the interior, and in so doing they gave Canada its name. The word 'kanata' was simply the Huron-Iroquois term for village. A river just north of Quebec City was named after Cartier and is a canoeing delight. It cuts into the ancient Canadian bedrock in the Jacques-Cartier Provincial Park, its rapids and waterfalls interspersed with placid sections. The environment shelters the grizzly bear, elk and other wildlife, in many parts remaining essentially unchanged from the time when native hunters scouted rivers and plains for easy prey.

Rivers empty into the Pacific and Arctic oceans, Hudson Bay, the Labrador Sea and the Atlantic Ocean. The immense Canadian Shield, the oldest part of the North American crustal plate, contains fossils of some of the earliest forms of life and bacteria from more than two billion years ago. To the west, the Northwest Territories, the Yukon and Alaska are ferociously rugged and isolated, with so much water that sometimes it is difficult to tell the difference between liquid and land.

THE TATSHENSHINI/ALSEK

A river guide giving the pretrip safety briefing to rafters on the Tatshenshini River in British Columbia advises them that they may struggle to breathe in the icy water. After a moment's silence during which this sobering information is absorbed, the guide adds that if you can't breathe it's probably because you have convulsively snatched a lungful before falling in. Your chest feels ready to burst because your throat clams up against the cold — you must breathe out first, in order to draw a breath in.

The Tatshenshini-Alsek Wilderness, straddling Canada and Alaska, is part of the world's largest protected area — 11 million hectares (27 million acres) containing a UNESCO World Heritage Site, and the Yukon's Kluane Reserve, which connects with Alaska's Wrangell-St Elias and Glacier Bay national parks. Rafting may be the only way to gain access, short of dropping in by parachute. An exciting 10-day trip covering 225km (140 miles) begins in British Columbia, with invigorating Class 3 rapids through the Tatshenshini Gorge. The river builds momentum as it winds toward the Alsek and Noisey mountain ranges, and

---

THE MISHTA-SHIPU (CHURCHILL) RIVER, CANADA

Developmental progress on rivers benefits some people but can be an onslaught on others. What some regard as a mere name is a symbol to others of how they are alienated from their past and isolated in the present. The Churchill River is a point in question: the largest river in Labrador, winding through the Canadian northeast towards the North Atlantic, carries the indigenous name of Mishta-shipu. In 1998 the governments of Quebec, Newfoundland and Labrador jointly announced the development of the Lower Churchill Falls hydroelectric project. However, according to the Innu people who claim aboriginal title and rights to the lands and waters, they had not been consulted. This was their homeland, which they called Nitassinan; it was not the first time the nomadic Innu people had been alienated from their land.

Before the 1970s, when they would trek by foot and canoe across their homeland, they used to look out for the gigantic falls of Patshetshunau, higher than Niagara by 25m (82ft). The name meant 'steam rising' and its clouds of mist could be seen for half a day's journey. On the maps, it was called the Churchill Falls. In 1953, the Newfoundland government gave rights to exploit the waters, forests and minerals of the Innu's Nitassinan to a private company in exchange for taxes and royalties – done without recognizing the rights of those who had lived there for countless generations, and who continued to depend on those lands for sustenance. In 1970 the Churchill Falls Dam was completed, flooding the upper portion of the Mishta-

shipu watershed to create the Smallwood reservoir. But upstream of the falls had been Michikamau Lake, an important seasonal hunting ground and meeting place for many Innu families. People returned one season in the early 1970s to find their canoes, snowshoes, traps, birth sites, buried ancestors, and land underwater. Says Tshaukuesh Penashue, an Innu woman, 'Every time I go on the bridge at Churchill Falls . . . I stop to show my grandchildren what happened . . . Under the bridge there's just rocks . . . there's no water . . . Lots of animals and fish died from the dam. . .'

Unfortunately the downstream stretch could suffer the same fate. The planned dam below Churchill Falls will flood large areas of shoreline habitat above Gull Island and Muskrat Falls. Abundant wildlife moves through the tall firs and is seen on some sandy beaches. Masked shrews, Arctic hares, deer mice, ermine, and beavers run through this wilderness, along with moose, caribou, black bears and wolves. And the five-day journey from below Churchill Falls to Goose Bay is popular with paddlers using open boats and traditional-style Indian canoes. Several Grade 2–3 rapids occur between stretches of fast but flat water.

The Innu people have never ceded any part of this land to any government, and despite complaints to the world's media, networking with similarly affected communities all over the globe, grievances published on the Internet, and demonstrations at the Quebec Parliament, the Innu have never won a hearing from the authorities.

becomes the Alsek River as it heads towards the Gulf of Alaska. An unrunnable canyon on the Alsek requires portage; but for the rest, the river difficulty rating of the Alsek is Class 3–4. The flow swells from an uncorrupted stream in a narrow canyon to a gigantic expanse of

moving water which seems to have cosmic proportions, where icebergs drift by like passing galaxies. Here, humans are rare, and on the edge of the flow, lush vegetation provides a habitat for wolves, bears, moose, mountain goats and eagles.

ABOVE: *The Tongass National Forest flanks the Alsek-Tatshenshini river system in the great cold northwest of North America. In the late fall, the river is low, breaking into braided streams between shoals of grey gravel.*

DOCTOR OF WHITEWATER, WALT BLACKADAR

Walt Blackadar, a medical doctor from Idaho, USA, ranks right up with the top paddlers in the annals of first descents. He kayaked – solo – Turnback Canyon on the remote and wild Alsek River in the Tatshenshini region of northern British Columbia. Commercial rafting trips take-out above the canyon and over it by helicopter to reach the safer lower Alsek. But not Walt Blackadar. On 25 August 1971, the ABC television show 'American Sportsman' captured his epic run down the canyon and projected him into millions of homes as the USA's first whitewater celebrity.

Blackadar only took up paddling in his forties. He was raised in New Jersey, graduated as a physician at Columbia University in 1946, and moved with his family to Salmon, Idaho, in 1949. Nearly two decades later he saw some eastern boaters running rapids around the Salmon and took up the sport himself.

There was not much to guide him, no-one knew much about kayaking, and most of the runs he did were first descents. He met and influenced a younger generation of paddlers. Tragedy first struck Blackadar when a young woman called Julie Wilson drowned while he was leading on the West Fork of the Bruneau River in Idaho. The episode haunted him; he was driven, too, by an obsession to run Devil's Creek Rapid on the Susitna, near Anchorage in Alaska. He never managed this successfully.

In 1978 Blackadar himself drowned on the South Fork of the Payette River, USA. The man who had run the Everest of kayaking, Turnback Canyon, floated nonchalantly into a log lying under the water, hit it hard, and slipped all the way under in his kayak. Held fast by the log, his boat folded over his back, he slid further into deeper water and finally his head disappeared. Death on the river, said one of his patients, was the right way for him to go.

SHOOTING THE HIGHEST FALLS

Ordinary boaters have been dumbstruck by the exploits of a few extremists who appear to know no limits. In 1996, British kayaker Shaun Baker ran the 19.7m (64ft) Aldeyjarfoss (falls) in Iceland, setting a recognized world record at the time.

An unofficial world record was set in 1987 by South African Corran Addison, when he kayaked over the 31m (101.68ft) Tignes Falls on the Isere River in the French Alps. It remained the highest fall run before the turn of the millennium, but was not recognized in the Guinness Book of Records because independent observers were not present.

By the end of the decade, the records were falling fast and furious. In 1998, a young woman from West Virginia called Shannon Carroll ran the 23.7m (78ft) Sahalie Falls on the McKenzie River near Eugene, Oregon, in the USA, taking the official world record. But a year later, 20-year-old Tao Berman, from Oregon, dropped 30m (98ft) off a waterfall on Johnson Creek, in Canada's Banff National Park. He broke his paddle but was uninjured, and said afterwards that he still had a few years to go. (As the saying amongst waterfallers goes: 'To air is human, to freefall divine'.)

Left: *The Tatshenshini River takes rafters through drifting icebergs in Canada and Alaska.*
Following Pages: *A kayaker is carried into the turmoil of Lava Falls Rapid on the Colorado River.*

NORTH AMERICA

THE SALMON, IDAHO

Perhaps the most significant river in North America, in rafting terms, is the feisty and picturesque Salmon in the state of Idaho, in far northwest America. It was first 'discovered' by the USA's most famous pair of explorers, Lewis and Clark. On 28 February 1803, President Thomas Jefferson won the approval of Congress to fund the Corps of Discovery on a mission to chart the West. Of course, American Indians (the First Nation) knew all about the rivers, but when Jefferson's secretary, Meriwether Lewis, and his friend William Clark set out, the West was terra incognita to the whites of the East.

Lewis and Clark completed an epic journey of more than 12,500km (8000 miles) to the Pacific coast, most of the way by river and much of it hard slog, dragging

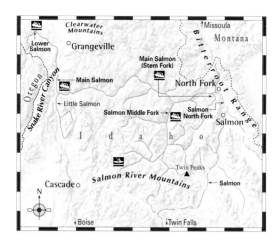

BELOW, LEFT TO RIGHT: *Rafters on the Salmon River, considered one of the USA's best whitewater rivers, has more than 100 rapids in 160km (100 miles). It was called the 'river of no return' because scows were sold at the end of the trip.*
OPPOSITE: *Flying spray – often icy – is a constant reminder of the treachery of turbulent waters.*

Main Salmon. The Class 3–4 rush through numerous chutes and 'golf courses' of many holes – such as Marble Creek, Haystack, Tappen Falls and House Rock – is accented by high water in June and July when the mountain runoff is at its maximum.

It is the Salmon's North Fork, overtopped by the striking Bitterroot Range, that is called River of No Return. In this mountainous wilderness, you could spot wildlife such as cougar, bear, otter, lynx, fox, beaver, badger, mink, mule deer and elk, and bighorn sheep and mountain goats stand watchfully in the meadows.

It was in this same general region that the rubber raft first made its appearance. The great 'pathfinder' of the American West was John Fremont. In 1843 he used a prototype inflatable, designed by fellow American Horace Day and patented by him in 1846, to probe the North Platte River in Wyoming State, just

and poling their boats upstream. They traced the course of the Missouri and ultimately reached the Salmon. Later the Salmon became known as the River of No Return, getting its name from boatmen who made one-way trips downriver and sold their wooden scows for scrap lumber before returning overland to Salmon City. In 1968, a century and a half after Lewis and Clark first

saw it, the Salmon was designated by Congress as amongst the first Wild and Scenic rivers to be protected by law, and to this day it remains undammed.

The Middle Fork of the Salmon is one of America's most loved alpine-style whitewater rivers. It comprises 170km (105 miles) of cascading rapids descending a total of 910m (3000ft) toward its confluence with the

east of Idaho. Fremont and his crew of seven chanced their luck on some fairly sizable rapids, enjoying themselves until they flipped on a rock and were pitched with all their provisions into the foam; this was the first recorded episode of what has become a common misfortune for the passengers of commercial rafting outfits.

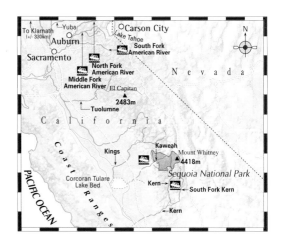

THE AMERICAN (NORTH AND MIDDLE FORK) AND OTHER RIVERS OF CALIFORNIA

Southwards in the warmer Sierra Nevada, shadowed by Mount Whitney (4418m; 14,495ft) and the Kaweah peaks, the Kaweah River runs along the southern entrance to Sequoia National Park. Like its boisterous neighbours the Kings, Tule and Kern rivers, it never actually reaches the Pacific Ocean but is soaked up by irrigation. However, the Kaweah has a reputation, in its upper reaches, as an intimidating Class 4+ run. It flows down the steepest drainage in California, producing continuous rapids with a dramatic backdrop of

snowcapped peaks and granite domes. Suicide Falls, Upper and Lower Slickies, and Holiday Hole are memorable in anyone's river lingo. Previous paddling experience is recommended and one should be in good physical shape and able to swim strongly.

The man who did more than anyone to put Class 5 rafting on the map is American Bill McGinnis, an English master's graduate who went into whitewater full-time in the 1970s. There was a time when all commercial trips were limited to Grade 3 (exciting but not technically difficult) rapids, but McGinnis and a few other operators changed all that. Hectic days in hefty whitewater are now the norm for experienced whitewater clients who have won their spurs on the easier routes and subsequently want to taste greater challenges. McGinnis wrote the 'Class Five Briefing' in the 1980s to prepare his guides mentally and technically for a much more testing experience than had hitherto been the norm.

Class 4–5 Californian rivers like the Klamath, the Salmon, Kaweah, Yuba and Stanislaus – to name some favourite staircases (rapids formed from continuous drops over boulders) – are now routinely attacked by teeth-gritting clients. Despite the higher level of risk, the safety record has remained good.

A cross-section of America's rivers reveals those that have had to be fought for, beach by beach, to preserve them from dam-builders or jealous landowners wanting the riverside outlook for themselves. The canyons of the American River in central California attract more than 700,000 visitors annually, and yet planners have talked of building a destructive dam at Auburn on the North and Middle forks of the river.

The American is a very long river that goes all the way from steep unrunnable crevices in the mountains around Lake Tahoe to the calm inner-tube and beer-bottle pools beside the trailer parks of Sacramento. The North Fork harbours a non-frivolous whitewater run whose ominous name, Giant Gap, says it all (verging on Class 5). Cliffs tower the height of several skyscrapers above the clear green river that smashes its way through boulder patches, finally running past mine tailings and cabin ruins from the gold rush of the 1850s.

The craziest human migration in history was ignited one cold morning in 1848 morning after a work crew found a few gold nuggets. Half a million frantic men and women flocked to California to plunder its yellow wealth. Most of them got nothing from the mother lode, and – like the characters in American movies –

THE TUOLUMNE BINDS TWO REMARKABLE MEN

many fell to disease, alcohol or bullets. Although nothing but ghosts remain, the echoes of their dynamite are still heard in the booming roar of the river itself at spots like Chamberlain Falls on the North Fork.

The Middle Fork has impressive rapids, including a big drop at Tunnel Chute Rapid where the river is first throttled in a narrow defile, only to rush underground for half the distance of a football field through a tunnel that was blasted by the gold miners long ago. It can all be rafted.

Further on is the ultimate Class 3 play run, called Chilli Bar, which is reliable in the daytime as it is dam-controlled. For this writer, the ethics of dam-building dependency aside, nothing compares. Chilli Bar is followed soon afterwards by the Gorge where a surfing wave can stand a boat on its nose forever.

LEFT: *The river slides over polished granite at The Slickies, on the rambunctious Kaweah River.*
ABOVE: *A series of pools and drops on the American River at Silver Fork.*
RIGHT: *Tuolumne (pronounced Too-all-o-me) River.*

California's protected Tuolumne River corridor seems to crackle with whitewater energy under the dry summer sun. Originating from snowmelt off mounts Dana and Lyell in Yosemite National Park, the Tuolumne drains through the Stanislaus National Forest. The main run starts at Cherry Creek and comprises 29km (18 miles) of almost continuous rapids including Nemesis, Thread-the-Needle, Hell's Kitchen and Pinball – none of them named to lend comfort to the nervous boater.

On this river in the late 1990s, two men from opposite ends of the earth, a Russian and a South African, met up – one in a raft, the other in a kayak. In the raft with three companions was the Russian, Vladimir Gavrilov, manager of the Tuolumne River operations for the outfitter Echo and a doctor of solid-state physics who felt it was better to be rafting. Gavrilov is one of the more influential river-runners of his generation. Author of an Internet book called Rivers of an Unknown Land, *Gavrilov had, during 27 years of whitewater explorations, run over 50 Grade 4 and 5 rivers in the former Soviet Republics. Since moving to the USA he had become a raft developer of note, taking Russian innovations in boat design forward into a new era of professional production.*

Just as remarkable was the man in the kayak. Willem van Riet, a South African landscape architect, was regarded as a pioneer of paddling routes on many of Southern Africa's major rivers (see p151), being the only person to have twice run the waterfall-strewn and crocodile-infested Kunene River on the border of Namibia and Angola. Van Riet had published a book in Afrikaans whose title translated as 'Downstream in My Canoe'. What was significant was that an international culture of river-running had brought together, in the heartland of American whitewater, two extraordinary individuals from two very different countries.

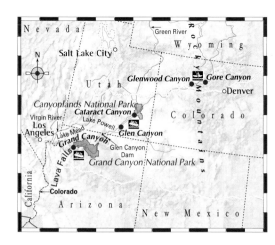

THE COLORADO, ARIZONA

Stand on the rim of the Grand Canyon of northern Arizona, away from the sightseers and the roads, and a faint rough whisper of rapids reaches you from below. This is the Colorado River churning through more than 160 rapids in a mile-deep trench. The legends of its monstrous rapids fuel modern river mythology everywhere. Enormous boat-munching 'holes' (where the current pours over rocks to roll back on itself with a washing-machine action) lurk at infamous rapids like Hance, Horn Creek, Granite and especially Lava Falls. Names like Phantom Ranch and Bright Angel Creek, Cheops Pyramid and The Tower of Ra, Peach Springs and Mooney Falls thrill the imagination, while if you catch sight of the strange creatures of the desert – collared and whiptail lizards, horned owls, rattlesnakes – they appear fixed like icons on the canyon's rocky outcrops.

Its reputation only seems to be enhanced by the fact that the canyon is an entirely managed environment – the river is dam-controlled, every access point is coming under increasing pressure from human numbers, and the experience of running the river is marketed as the ultimate Disneyland of whitewater. By comparison with the Grand Canyon, the canyons of the Tsangpo (in Tibet) and Colca (Peru) are far deeper; and the volume of the Victoria Nile in Uganda averages at least 10 times that of the Colorado. From the Himalayas to New Zealand, scores of far more challenging rivers are being plied by commercial operators as the international rafting boom continues. Yet, many boaters would agree that to run the Grand Canyon is to become a member of a special clan of people, and is close to being a mystical experience.

RIGHT: *A dory runs Cataract Canyon on the Colorado River, Utah, during flood conditions.*

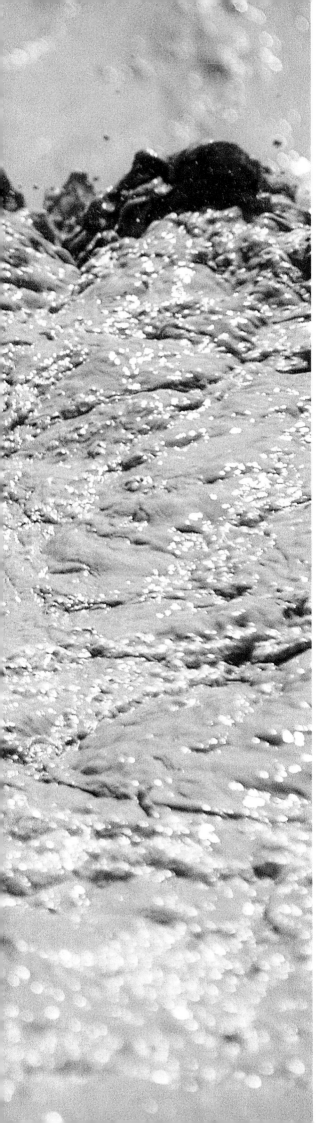

Limits on the numbers of private trippers are a source of some frustration for the many who dream of the untrammelled freedom enjoyed by boaters of yore. Of the 22,000 people allowed on the Colorado River each year, more than 80 per cent book through operators who hold concessions from the National Parks Service. At the start of the new millennium, the list of applications for private trips through the Grand Canyon National Park had about 7000 people on it with an estimated wait of 12 years. Fortunately the list drops about 300 to 500 a year due to cancellations, so the chances of going far sooner increase.

The Grand Canyon is the highlight of the Colorado's long rapid-strewn course. The upper Colorado, in Colorado State, runs through two very exciting canyons, Gore and Glenwood. The extremely taxing annual Gore Canyon whitewater race is held over a technical 8km (5-mile) run which includes at least half a dozen Class 5 rapids and so attracts gung-ho paddling talent, with plenty of spectator value for those who come to witness major wipe-outs. Glenwood Canyon is intersected at several points by the I-70 highway, a spectacular engineering feat sculpted into the red cliffs; this makes viewing access easy but can reduce the enjoyment of floaters on the river as they pass beneath whirring cameras. No matter — further down, the river enters serpentine declivities well off the beaten track: Horsethief and Ruby Canyons, Westwater Canyon, and then the big one, Cataract Canyon, which proffers outstanding 'big water' trips through the Canyonlands National Park in the state of Utah. The Colorado's main tributary, the Green, joins it here in a landscape increasingly arid and lonely. Rainfall all but ceases and the waters become increasingly salty due to evaporation and runoff from natural salt beds that were once at the bottom of an ancient sea.

By the time the Colorado River reaches the Grand Canyon it is a mere 300m (980ft) above sea level. It now loses the rest of its elevation in a series of giant steps down, battering its way between rocks that were formed in relatively recent geological times. Within the past six million years the land began to rise or warp upwards, and the river commenced down-cutting, following its ancient meanders to create incredible hairpin-bend gorges. Nine successive bands of rock account for the glorious multicoloured layering effect of the canyon — black, red, brown, lavender, grey, white and red. At the lowest levels beside the river are Precambrian schists and gneisses, above them are Cambrian sandstones, shales and limestones. Next up are the Redwall cliffs of the Mississippian period. The topmost layers are more shales and sandstones of the Supai formation, and right on top are the Coconino sandstones and Kaibab limestones. Cross-cutting dykes, landslide piles and lava flows form many of the rapids.

Passing down these rock corridors, year-long, in vibrant sunlight or cold wintry noons, rafts and kayaks carry their wondering passengers into a land painted with an ochrous brush. By world whitewater standards, the Colorado rapids feature mountainous waves, but they are fairly straightforward in boating terms. When the river rises after heavy winter snows, it becomes a much more threatening prospect, with big holes and mighty wave trains capable of flipping the biggest rafts. Modern raftmasters belonging to the Grand Canyon River Guides Association are a privileged few who have managed to secure themselves positions on the river where everyone wants to work and play. They are exceedingly well-versed in the history and geology of the region, and even more so in how to deal with capsizes and catch flotsam in the rapids. Commercial operators, of whom there are just over a dozen holding concessions from the National Parks Service, hasten to reassure possible clients that their safety and comfort is paramount and they can always get out and walk around the worst rapids.

OARSMEN OF THE PAST

The story of Colorado boating marks a steady progression from heroism to holism. The first to confront the river were men of unflinching character. A one-armed geology professor, John Wesley Powell, led a surveying party down the Grand Canyon in 1869 in clumsy wooden boats with the official object of charting it (though his self-confessed pleasure was to dodge merrily amongst the rocks and waves). His story is well known, and his Diary of the First Trip through the Grand Canyon is a classic of adventure literature, vividly describing the sweeping, violent progress of the river and the fears of the men.

LEFT: *A swimmer finds out what it means to capsize and take a bath in the muddy and turbulent waters of the Colorado, Grand Canyon.*

The Upper Gorge Canyon, near the source of the Colorado River, offers high-grade rafting at its best – and scariest. This is for tough, experienced paddlers only.

A kayaker in a touring kayak slips over the lip of a scary drop on the Gunnison River in Colorado.

Powell's expedition started on the Green River in Wyoming, met the Colorado above formidable Cataract Canyon in Utah, and from there proceeded all the way through the Grand Canyon to the confluence with the Virgin River in California. Powell's achievement is usually depicted as an isolated feat. Yet he charted the canyon at the very time that Henry Morton Stanley was crossing Central Africa by boat on the Congo River. Dr David Livingstone had already explored the Zambezi and Shire rivers in Southern Africa in his quest to end the slave trade. And the existence of the Grand Canyon had been known to the Spaniards for three centuries since 1540, when the explorer Francisco Vasquez de Coronado led an expedition from Mexico (New Spain) into the interior. Perhaps what is surprising about Powell's journey is that it happened relatively late in the opening up of the American West; evidence enough that the Grand Canyon was feared and avoided by all.

RIVER OF 'FIRSTS'

The first man to run every rapid on the Grand Canyon solo was Buzz Holmstrom. In 1937 this unassuming pump station attendant from Coquille, Oregon, completed the trip solo in an oarboat, and not satisfied, he returned the following year to run every single rapid. He summed up the appeal of the river by saying that it 'demands respect and will punish those who do not treat it properly'. In his view, anyone whom the Colorado allowed through its canyons to see its wonders should feel thankful and privileged.

The first commercial tour operator on the Grand Canyon was also the first woman river guide, Georgie White, known as Woman of the Rivers. She started conducting trips in 1947 using a motorized triple-rig raft. White first swam 97km (60 miles) of the lower canyon in 1945 and then, lashing military surplus inflatables together to make a three-raft platform, she started charging anything from US$50 to US$100 – whatever visitors were prepared to pay – for a trip. She made it possible for more people to enjoy the rapids, rafting in comparative safety, though her contribution was not universally admired by those who believed the Grand Canyon should stay free of engines and crowds. Women-only trips on the Grand Canyon started in the 1970s with an emphasis on the uplifting and nurturing role of rivers rather than the raw provocation of rapids.

The Colorado was probably the first major river to have someone swim all the rapids 'just for a lark'. In 1955 Bill Beer and his friend John Daggett donned rubber shirts, Mae West life jackets, long underwear and fins to swim unassisted in the bone-chilling water from Lees Ferry to Lake Mead. It was illegal even then. The authorities finally softened when they realized these two young adventurers were somewhat crazed but entirely dedicated to their mission, and allowed them to finish. Their underwear in tatters, their limbs chafed by the cords they had tied to themselves to tow along two army surplus sealed boxes each, Beer and Daggett staggered out at Pierce Ferry as freakish national heroes.

TAMING OF A RIVER

The Colorado is impounded upstream at the Glen Canyon Dam, built in 1964, which forms Lake Powell, and downstream at the Hoover, or Boulder Dam, built between 1931–36, to form Lake Mead. Due to excessive draw-offs, the mighty Colorado dries up before reaching the sea, where its estuary becomes dismal cracked mudflats. This is a sad fate for the Colorado, at 2330km (1450 miles) the longest river in North America west of the Rocky Mountains. The Spaniards named it the river that was 'coloured red'; but since the dams capture most of its silt load, it is now grey-green as it flows out below Glen Canyon.

The disbelief with which the building of Glen Canyon was greeted was best expressed by folksinger-actress Katie Lee, who alternated her stage career with that of professional river guide. She liked to be called 'the Mistress of the River' and entitled her autobiography *All My Rivers Are Gone*. Beginning in 1953 when Georgie White was already operating, Lee ran at least 16 trips down the Glen Canyon gorge, giving names to some of its side canyons, but after the dam wall went up she never again floated the river.

The Grand Canyon is one of the original homelands of America's 'first nation'. From about 11,000 years ago, Paleo-Indians settled in the region. Gradually they evolved into the Archaic people, hunter-gatherers who left behind charms made of willow twigs, with which they appear to have magically invoked the spirits of their animal prey. More recently, the Hopis, Paiutes and Navajos avoided using the river as a

canoeing route as they regarded it with superstitious awe. The Havasupai tribe presently occupies the main reservation on the river and its members consider themselves the traditional guardians of the flat-topped mesas, vanishing ravines, and blue-green waterfalls that tumble into the canyon.

A river that commanded the hearts and minds of river-runners worldwide, one of the gurus of the Sixties Generation, Edward Abbey, kept a journal of a dory trip through the Grand Canyon in 1977, and in it he wrote:

'Night and day the river flows. If time is the mind of space, the river is the soul of the desert. Brave boatmen come, they go, they die, the voyage flows on forever. We are all canyoneers. We are all passengers on this little mossy ship, this delicate dory sailing round the sun that humans call the earth. Joy, shipmates, joy.'

(*The Hidden Canyon — A River Journey*)

THE OCOEE, TENNESSEE

Across the other side of the USA is a favourite of rafters and kayakers, the Ocoee River in eastern Tennessee, which is intensively managed as a

BELOW: *A canoeist, kneeling and using a single-bladed paddle, surfs a hole on the Ocoee River.*

whitewater playground. It is one of the most action-packed short runs in the world. The 1996 Atlanta Olympic slalom course was built at the top of the gorge, and on the commercial rafting run are miles of great rapids culminating in the world-class river rodeo site known as the Hell Hole. With its sparkling water and overhanging greenery, the Ocoee is a Disneyland of wet and wonderful fun, attracting more than 2000 river-runners per day on average.

The Ocoee flows in a rough granite and dolomite stream bed formed by the collision of two continental plates. In 1909 its water was diverted into massive wooden flumes, or channels, for the generation of hydroelectric power; and for nearly 70 years the riverbed was empty, choked with weeds, boulders and trees. In 1984 a contract was negotiated with Tennessee Valley Authority (TVA) officials, providing for whitewater releases and bringing money to the county.

The river only runs at scheduled release times, with rafting companies paying a couple of dollars a head for the use of the water to compensate for loss of hydro power. It flows for 116 days of the year, mostly in high summer, but not on Tuesdays and Wednesdays, which are for hydro generation. Overnight and on nonrafting days, the riverbed is dry but for the pools left by the previous day's surge.

On flow days, the scene at the top of the Ocoee run is quite extraordinary. At 08:00, not a soul is seen in the huge parking lot. Then the buses arrive, stacked high with rafts on roofracks. All day, the buses will grind up and down the narrow tarred road beside the river, returning the rafts and dropping off squads of tourists clad in life jackets and helmets.

At 09:00, a rush of whitewater pours over the low-head dam near the parking lot. The army of rafters marches down a slipway to launch into the sudden deluge, heading off at the rate of one raft every 10–30 seconds with six to 12 people on board.

The run takes a maximum of three hours, and the first whitewater blast occurs immediately – a big Grade 4 rapid where the unwary take their first swim. Excitement is closely packed thereafter. To name only a few hot-spots: Double Suck, Double Trouble, Table Saw, Hell Hole, and finally, Bubba Home Free.

The Ocoee Valley has a history of enforced removals and loss of spiritual territory. Hundreds of years ago, the Catawba Indians, or 'people of the river', lived peacefully around the Ocoee, whose name meant 'place of the Catawba'. From around 1500, invaders known as the Cherokee – or 'people of different speech' – overpowered the Creek Indians. They took up residence in today's Cherokee National Forest. The Cherokee people themselves endured a time of great sorrow when many of them lost their land during the early 1800s to enforced removal as well as to white frontier settlement

DARING EXTREMISTS OF THE POTOMAC

The Potomac River basin in West Virginia, in the eastern USA, holds the earliest evidence of inhabited structures in North America; it was a boundary between North and South in the Civil War, and is home to the USA's seat of government.

A race on the Potomac that used to follow a 13km (8-mile) run through Wet Bottom Chute, Maryland Chute at Difficult Run, Yellow Falls, and Stubblefield Falls has, over the years, gone from being a challenge for experts to an easy run for intermediate boaters; today it is a family race, with safety boats laid on. But it is not this family race that attracts the 'hairboaters' (those who run wild rapids where the spray literally resembles hair streaming off the waves). Rather, a daunting prospect to daredevil kayakers is the Great Falls of the Potomac River outside Washington DC. Extremists run the main falls, where the river plops over a series of steps considered to be the most dramatic natural landmark in the nation's capital. A 23m (76ft) drop over about 1.6km (1 mile) creates the biggest runnable rapids in the eastern USA. In 1998 a top American kayaker, Scott Bristow (at left), dropped into the notorious Charlie's Hole backwards and disappeared. His body was never found. A small error in setting up for his line over the drop may have caused this accident, confirming what local paddlers have said before: that running waterfalls is always dangerous, and even the best can miscalculate.

– and on their way to a government resettlement area in Oklahoma, died as a result of a lack of facilities, inadequate shelter and supplies, and disease.

THE NEW, WEST VIRGINIA

Moving northwards to West Virginia, the Appalachian mountain chain yields a couple of notable whitewater attractions. The New River bubbles up in the Blue Ridge Mountains and gushes along for 400km (250 miles) through mountains, rolling hills and farmland to the forested slopes of West Virginia's coal country. The Gauley River joins it below Fayetteville. The world's longest single-arch steel-span bridge swoops gracefully across the New Gorge some 267m (876ft) above the water, and on Bridge Day every October, river rafters are treated to the sight of BASE jumpers parachuting off into oblivion. The rivers, too, are not for the faint-hearted.

Despite its name, the New River is the oldest in North America, estimated at 320 million years, meaning that the Appalachians have risen up around it. The New would have formed part of an immense lake or tropical swamp; inklings of that warm past remain as, once one is past the cold air in the shaded gorge, the river picks up several warm water tributaries, making it unusually balmy to the skin.

A majestic canyon situated between the towns of Hinton and Fayetteville has been conserved, since 1978, as the New River Gorge National River. Here the New has become known as the Grand Canyon of the eastern USA.

First boated for pleasure in 1969, it offers Class 1 to 5 rapids, starting with milder action on the Upper New but leading to serious runs on the Lower. The water funnels down between the 300m-high (1000ft) walls, creating pool-and-drop configurations that allow for short

breathers between bouts of combat. Do not be put off by the terrified screams of fellow rafters, who may be screaming with fear – or just for effect.

The Gauley River, if anything, is worse, and beginning as it does in the misted thunder of the outflow from the Summersville Dam, it is about as close as one will ever come to an experience of Dante's Hell with high humidity. A rapid named Insignificant is not; Pillow Rock is not a good spot for a relaxing snooze; and all in all the 23km (14 miles) of the trip are best described in the local lingo as a 'hootenanny with a hairy river'.

BELOW: *A paddler tackles the foaming waters of the New River in West Virginia.*
OPPOSITE: *Scott Bristow flys off Pummel at the Great Falls of the Potomac River near Washington DC.*

CENTRAL & SOUTH AMERICA

PACUARE * AMAZON * ORINOCO * COLCA * FUTALEUFU

The mother of all rivers has many children – many tributaries run together into the Amazon, some springing from the snowfields of the Andes around Lake Titicaca or cascading down its wet eastern slopes through Bolivia, Peru, Colombia and Ecuador. Some spill from the Guiana Highlands of Venezuela and some snake from the plateau of the Mato Grosso in southern Brazil, down through muggy rainforest into the great basin of the mother river itself, the Amazon.

Other great rivers in South and Central America promise adventure on a limitless scale; and indeed the region was 'discovered' by kayakers and rafters from the late 1970s onwards, and is today firmly on the map of world whitewater 'musts'. From the cloud forests of Costa Rica to the fjord-land of Chile, the fourth largest continent offers some of the cleanest and most spectacular rivers in existence, their aquamarine waters tumbling below pinnacles of ice-sheathed rock and skirting round the foot of still-active volcanoes. The highest mountain in the Western Hemisphere is a volcano, Mt Aconcagua (6960m; 22,834ft). Situated in western Argentina,

it stands starkly against the skyline, visible to kayakers on the river of the same name which flows westward through the Chilean coastal forest to enter the Pacific Ocean near Valparaiso.

As much as its rivers and mountains, the attraction of South and Central America resides in the region's rich blend of original Andean, Inca, Aztec, and colonial Spanish and Portuguese cultures. Visitors encounter the timeless habits and infinite patience of people who have lived for generations with military dictatorships and endemic terrorism, both frequently fuelled by drug production. Despite this, people retain their optimism and do sometimes succeed in re-establishing democracy and law. Tour buses bounce along wild hairpin tracks, passing through untidy and yet soulful villages perched on rain-eroded ridges. Everywhere in the Andes is the indigenous beast of burden, the llama, its lidded eyes beholding life with a superior gaze as it lopes along with a strange gawky gait carrying produce to market.

Into this most esoteric of new worlds came the paddlers. South America's whitewater canyons often combine exhilarating rapids with awesome scenery.

ABOVE, LEFT TO RIGHT: *Heart-thumping excitement awaits boaters on the Urubamba River, flowing through the Sacred Valley of the Inca, near Cuzco, Peru; a waterfall plunges straight into the Bío-Bío River in central Chile as boaters drift by; to get to the Colca River, rafters have to scramble down the canyon's 2000m-high (6560ft) cliff slopes.*
OPPOSITE: *A kayaker hurtles into the maelstrom of the Futaleufu River (or Fu, as it is fondly known), in southern Chile.*

THE PACUARE, COSTA RICA

Costa Rica is a small country in Central America, with only a day's drive separating Panama, to the south, from the country's northern border with Nicaragua, but in this small compass is a knot of steaming volcanoes, forested mountains, lowland jungles and rolling savannahs.

The Pacuare River flows from Costa Rica's central highlands into the Caribbean Sea. It is almost impossible to capture the sense of opulent, earthy fertility that makes this river so special. It rises in cloud forest and drops through hills musty with the smell of humus. Some 850 species of birds have been counted, including toucans and tanagers. The strange names of the wildlife confirm the uniqueness of the landscape, for you will find here armadillos, sloths, peccaries, agoutis, and coati-mundis, sharing the forest depths with mink-coated monkeys and the most bizarre collection of colourful butterflies.

A section of the Pacuare has been declared a protected area by the Costa Rican government, giving it the status of a Wild and Scenic River. Its emerald-green whitewater is fed by numerous side creeks where bathers can dip into the plunge pools beneath graceful waterfalls, as they pause between rafting the rapids. The rapids match the 'wild' designation of the river. It has an upper (Class 5) section for those known as seasoned jungle 'hairboaters', with easier sections below. Some 50km (32 miles) of Class 3–4 rapids are linked by tranquil pools. Apart from the thrill-seekers, the Pacuare was also the venue for the 1998 downriver

kayak race which forms part of the Camel Whitewater Challenge events. The race format consisted of one kayak discipline, and three rafting disciplines undertaken on the nearby Reventazon: Raft Sprint, Raft Slalom, Raft Downriver and Kayak Downriver. Wide-eyed competitors emerged battered and bruised at the finish of the kayak race to confess that rock dodging in the Pacuare had come as a testing surprise after the far easier runs on Africa's Zambezi River.

Raft racers were disappointed to learn that the Reventazon was to be dammed in its most exciting section in the future. The Reventazon is a bigger volume river than the Pacuare, thus more suitable for rafting. At the time it had three major whitewater sections: the relatively easy Power House run (Class 3), the tougher Pascua section (Class 4), and the tense Peralta rapids (Class 5) for which only the tough and experienced should apply. Although it was Peralta where the championship downriver races and raft heats took place, this section has now gone under water, leaving the less strenuous parts. At the time, the teams once again found the river far more difficult than the Zambezi, with continuous rapids that were shallower and more technical.

Both rivers flow eastwards to join the Caribbean Sea north of the city of Limón, an area with a low-density human population. The wilder, more protected areas of Costa Rica lie further to the south, in the Talamanca Mountains extending into Panama. Here, too, many rivers pour down the flanks of notable peaks such as Chirripó (3819m; 12,530ft), where a national park is home to many animals. Of Costa Rica's rich indigenous wildlife, the jaguar, ocelot, tapir and tinamu still found in the wild hills of the Reventazon and Pacuare catchments could be endangered as a result of the rivers destined for development. In due course, endangered wildlife may find sanctuary only in the protected areas.

Dams or not, Costa Rica remains a whitewater paradise – especially so as its warm rivers reach their best in October–December when others in the Northern Hemisphere are iced up or very low.

OPPOSITE: The normally wild Pacuare River in Costa Rica – which was the scene of the kayaking event in the 1998 world rafting championship (Camel Whitewater Challenge) – is seen here in a fairly placid stretch as competitors take a 'friendship float' after the races.

BURNING THE FORESTS

Before European settlement, at least three million Indians lived in the forests of Brazil alone. Today that number has dwindled to 225,000 due to disease and dispossession. Their lives revolved around the rivers. They ate manatees, dolphins, turtles and their eggs, which were laid by the hundreds on the sandy shores of the rivers. In the remoter areas they can still be seen living in huts thatched with wide leaves or reeds, sleeping in hammocks, and paddling in dugout canoes.

Today it is a region under threat from burning, deforestation and, ultimately, even the encroachment of desert conditions. Once the tree cover is stripped away, the soils tend to be poor and they do not support intensive agriculture. The bare land reflects back the heat of the sun and dries out the atmosphere.

Environmentalists and the South American Indians are working together to stop deforestation and to create markets for products such as nuts, fruits, oils, and pigments that can be harvested without destroying the forest.

In the late 1980s the Amazon rainforests drew international attention when an environmental activist, Chico Mendes, was assassinated. He had campaigned against the burning of the forests by farmers and ranchers, and he paid the ultimate price. The battle did not end there. At the Earth Summit in Rio de Janeiro, Brazil, a few years later, the nations of the world made a commitment to protect the rainforests, and although some have not lived up to their promises, the issue is at least on the agenda.

THE AMAZON, BRAZIL

The Amazon is navigable for almost its entire length — ocean-going ships can sail from the Atlantic all the way to the city of Iquitos at the foot of the Andes in the extreme west of the country, making it an important commercial route across the jungle — but this means that, in terms of whitewater, there simply is none. Recreational boating on the Amazon is in the nature of sightseeing and rainforest educational tours. But if one penetrates the higher reaches, rapids abound. The Apurimac — the highest and longest source of the Amazon — was first boated from its source to the sea in 1983, and later swum by a hardy adventurer using a riverboard all the way to the Atlantic Ocean. Oddly enough, playing a leading role in these contemporary epics were South Africans, who have made South America their second adventure home.

The extraordinary position of the Andes, one of the world's greatest mountain ranges squeezed along the Pacific coastal spine of the South American continent, has made the Amazon basin what it is. Composed of sedimentary rocks compacted by gargantuan folding and topped off by active volcanoes, the Andes have an average breadth of only 240km (150 miles), and yet they dominate a low-lying region that, a few degrees south of the Equator, is about 3000km (1900 miles) in length and half again as wide. The mountain rampart sits on the edge of this vast plain which lies at close to sea level, and into which pour the principal rivers. Each is a major world waterway in its own right: the Xingu, Tapajós, Madeira, Purus and Juruá entering from the south; the Ucayali, Marañón and Napo rivers from the west; and the Putumayo, Japurá and Negro from the north. The fact that most of these names are unfamiliar in the world outside testifies to the overwhelming reputation of the one river we all know.

The main course of the Amazon is so broad there are no bridges across it. It has the world's biggest outflow at the sea, equalling that of more than 600 Colorado rivers. It is not quite the longest river at 6437km (4000 miles), since that distinction goes to the 6741km (4187-mile) Nile. The basin of the Amazon is next only to the ocean in its concentration of life on this planet, holding 40 per cent of the world's leaf-bearing forests which, through transpiration, make the largest contribution of the land to the Earth's oxygen supply.

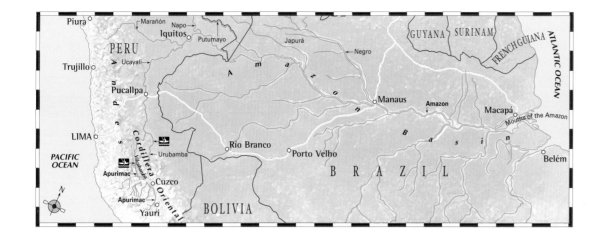

APURIMAC — TACKLING A TRIBUTARY

The highest and longest source of the Amazon River is the Apurimac, rising in south-central Peru at Lake Villafro, and following a northern course to unite with the Urubamba River. The Apurimac, mused Californian adventurer Joe Kane, was 'not a civilized river'. In the native Quechua language, the word means 'speaker of the gods'. It runs through a sacred valley below Cuzco, a town in the Cordillera Oriental of the Andes, and along its course are few villages and fewer bridges. Roads cross the river only eight times — and they are terrible crossings. For miles at a time the gorge is more than 3000m (9850ft) deep, and down on the boulder-strewn floor the river's sheer velocity overwhelms all other life. The turbulent section between Yauri and Peru's San Francisco is most dangerous in the narrow passages, where the risk of entrapment by the pounding water is high.

The Apurimac thaws reluctantly from a dessicated snowfield, becomes a rivulet of clear water, and grows incessantly as it crosses flat pampas (grassy plains) between windswept hills. At 4000m (13,100ft) the Apurimac begins one of the most spectacular descents of any river in the world, slicing into the Vilcabamba mountain range and pushing through canyons where the light hardly shines, on its way toward the jungle.

This is the inhospitable ravine that beckoned a Utah University professor, J Calvin Giddings. He led the first navigation of the river in 1974 and 1975. As he only wrote it up and published it in 1996 shortly before his death, his achievement went virtually unknown for two decades. By the time his book *Demon River Apurimac* appeared, Giddings' reputation as a chemist specializing in chromatography was well established and colleagues were surprised to learn about his unique voyage. Giddings had explored many high-class western-river whitewater runs back in the days when they were nearly all new. His interest then turned to the Apurimac, where he did two trips.

The first, in 1974, attempted to trace the course of the topmost water that could be paddled, starting within sight of 6000m (19,700ft) peaks. However, following several nightmarish days battling against wild rapids, Giddings had to abandon the trip after 65km (40 miles). A year later, he was back with a group of five friends, going in 115km (70 miles) below the previous take-out and completing the course.

Today the safer reaches of the Apurimac are commercially rafted, along with the waters of other Amazon tributaries: the Urubamba, Huaran, Río Tambopata and Río Majés. Modern maps, river know-how and improved state-of-the-art equipment have all conspired to make rafting and kayaking in this region a relatively safe and accessible option for tourists on the Inca trail. A trip brochure expounds on Class 5 rapids that have names like Toothache, and Your First and Last Laugh.

CONQUERING THE MIGHTY AMAZON

Until 1986, the Amazon had never been done from source to sea. Then 10 men and one woman from around the world, initially led by South Africans, set out to do so on foot, by raft and in kayaks. The expedition took six months and was seriously marred by acrimonious fallouts. Finally, only two, a Polish paddler named Piotr Chmielinski and Californian Joe Kane, finished the trip. Kane went on to write the story of this flawed expedition in his book *Running the Amazon*, which quickly established itself as a classic of modern adventure.

OPPOSITE: *The Amazon rainforest burns.*
BELOW: *Gasping for breath, Tim Biggs executes a roll on the Apurimac during his 1985 expedition.*

It was to the mountain stronghold of Mount Mismi, which marks the source of the Amazon's furthest tributary, the Apurimac, and overlooks the desolate altiplano (elevated plains) of the Andes, that a young adventurer came in August 1997. South African-born Mike Horn arrived with a paraglider and a strange-looking boat, something that looked like a cross between a surfboard and a canoe — a hydrospeed.

Much favoured by French daredevils, the hydrospeed is a derivative of the boogie board, used on ocean waves. Instead of surfing down the face of waves, however, the hydrospeed goes through them. It is basically a reinforced riverboard allowing you to punch through the rapid as your finned feet propel you forward bodily into the heart of the whitewater. Mike Horn had climbed from a Pacific beach in Camana, Peru, and now launched himself off the summit of Mount Mismi. The hydrospeed, filled with food and provisions, was strapped to Horn's back as he took a daring leap of faith and paraglided across the high snowfields towards his landfall on the banks of the Apurimac River. Incredible as it sounds, Horn was about to make the first solo crossing of South America on foot and water. His aim was to swim virtually the full length of the Amazon lying on the hydrospeed. And he succeeded.

Horn spent years planning every detail of the Amazon trip and perfecting his hydrospeed technique. By the time he hit the river he had survived at least one near-drowning in the Alps and was one of the world's foremost exponents of whitewater rafting. His decision to start his journey by paraglider was taken after reading reports by paddlers who described the trickle of the river in its early stages. As it drops more than 4000m (9840ft) in about 500km (310 miles), he decided to skip the impassable shallows and set off on the river voyage when there was enough water to start kicking with his fins.

Seven months later, having braved the cold, survived the violent rapids of the Apurimac, escaped anti-drug vigilantes, and avoided the crocodiles and the piranha of the main Amazon, Horn reached the mouth of the river — only to be beaten back by the tidal bore rushing

RIGHT: *Piotr Chmielinski (USA) at the source of the Amazon, August 1985. He successfully navigated the entire length of the Amazon in six months.*

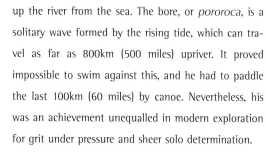

PUSHING THE LIMITS IN SOUTH AMERICA

In the late 1990s, as South America became the new mecca for kayaking playboaters and radical rafters, fatal accidents began to happen here as they did in other parts of the world. Snake-hissing Class 5 rapids are nerve-wracking but exhilarating for those who successfully run them, yet there is no guarantee of survival if you come adrift in them.

Ecuador, bordered by Colombia to the northeast and Peru to the south and east, has two chains of the Andes, the Cordillera Occidental and Cordillera Oriental, marking off the high Sierra, or central highlands. One of the highest active volcanoes in the world, Cotopaxi (5897m; 19,350ft), is located between the two mountain chains. Here the many headwaters of the Napo River converge to meet the Amazon in Peru after crossing the Oriente (eastern jungle) on the Cordillera Oriental.

The rivers of the Quijos valley in the Cordillera Oriental, near the town of Tena, have a special feel to them: the air is relatively less humid and there are fewer bugs than in lower-lying parts of the country. The region is a natural drawcard for river-runners. It was in this jungle on the gently declining eastern slopes of the Cordillera that a young kayaker from Tennessee, USA, Steve Stone, met his death in January 1998. He was a competent but very independent boater who insisted on paddling ahead and alone. He had linked up informally with a kayaking group comprising a raft guide and friends who boated together on the Río Hollin and Río Misahualli. Highlights of the Class 4+ Hollin are the Sumaco waterfall and a chance to paddle through a cave.

Stone vanished over the horizon line of a drop and when his companions finally caught up with his lifeless body in a hole at the bottom, they tried in vain to revive him with cardiopulmonary resuscitation. They later saw that Stone's helmet had a very serious impact just above his right ear and speculated he had been knocked unconscious as he plunged over the fall. Stone's death was one of many rafting tragedies recorded annually in the US Whitewater Accident Report prepared by American Whitewater (AWA) and freely available as a safety service on the Internet. At the end of the 1990s, even exceptionally skilled boaters were dying as they pushed the limits of the possible.

With training on their side, adventurers seem able to defy the forces of nature only because they have carefully calculated the outcomes. For them, risk and real values coincide. If the world's great rivers taught us anything in the closing years of the 20th century, it is that we can push out the limits of the possible if we restrain the impulse to prove that absolutely anything is possible, never mind the risk.

up the river from the sea. The bore, or *pororoca*, is a solitary wave formed by the rising tide, which can travel as far as 800km (500 miles) upriver. It proved impossible to swim against this, and he had to paddle the last 100km (60 miles) by canoe. Nevertheless, his was an achievement unequalled in modern exploration for grit under pressure and sheer solo determination.

While journeying down the Apurimac abyss (which appears on some maps as the upper Amazon), Horn ruefully echoed the findings of earlier kayakers and rafters. They had complained that the bombardment of rocks from above — dislodged by natural erosion — made them fear for their lives. More life-threatening situations followed when he entered the infamous Red Zone, a stretch of river between San Francisco (Peru) and Atalaya. The Indians living in the jungle here regard drug traffickers as a menace to their legal crops of manioc, and they are inclined to shoot strangers on sight. Horn managed to dodge bullets although he was detained several times. He was finally released when an inadvertent triggering of his satellite-driven SOS device attracted a Peruvian military helicopter.

Along the way, as Horn entered warmer, crocodile-infested waters, he avoided the riverbanks during the hottest hours of the day. The Amazon's renowned freshwater 'pink dolphin' were friendly companions, appearing several times on his journey, drawn by curiosity to investigate the vibrations of the flippers. Horn shared the water with piranha (who generally only attack a person with an open wound), stingrays, sawfish and sharks. Finally in January 1998, Horn stood triumphantly on the shores of the Atlantic.

On returning to his wife and children in Switzerland, Horn became a motivational speaker much in demand by bankers and businessmen of the corporate world.

As this book was written, Horn had just completed a solo odyssey around the world that took him back to the Amazon. He followed latitude 0 along the equator, passing over three oceans, across numerous islands and across two continents, South America and Africa. His feat won him The Laureus World Sports Award for the Alternative Sportsperson of the Year.

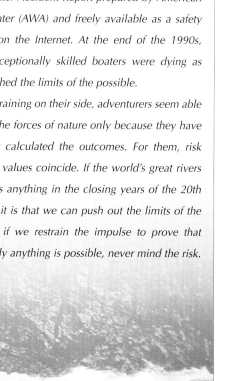

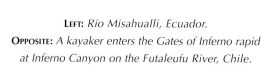

LEFT: *Río Misahualli, Ecuador.*
OPPOSITE: *A kayaker enters the Gates of Inferno rapid at Inferno Canyon on the Futaleufu River, Chile.*

THE ORINOCO, VENEZUELA

The Orinoco River, which has its birthplace in the Guiana Highlands, and the Amazon, originating in the Andes, share the singular distinction among the world's great rivers of being connected by a flowing channel. Known as the Casiquiare Canal, it is a natural rather than a man-made channel.

The Casiquiare leaves the Orinoco at Tamatama and joins the Río Negro, the biggest tributary of the Amazon, some 335km (210 miles) later after meandering through a particularly bug-infested section of the Amazon Basin.

In the early 1980s a father and son team achieved one of the greatest canoeing triumphs on record by using the Casiquiare Canal to complete a madcap journey between Lake Winnipeg in North America and the mouth of the Amazon. Canadian Don Starkell and his son Dana ended their two-year odyssey in May 1982, arriving at Belem in the Amazon delta in a kind of 'unbelieving numbness'. They had launched on the Red River, Winnipeg. Thence they paddled downstream to the Minnesota River in the USA to join the broad Mississippi.

From the Mississippi delta in Louisiana they carried on in the open sea around the Gulf of Mexico, nearly

THE BÍO-BÍO, CHILE

Moving south to Chile, the central Andes become narrower and lower (for a time) than in the north, and here the high plateau gives way to a valley nearly 1000km (600 miles) long and between 40 and 80km (25 and 50 miles) wide. It is the most populous part of Chile. It is a fertile area, dominated by the peak of Aconcagua and skirted in the south by the Bío-Bío River. It is the first of the Chilean rivers to have become world renowned – at least amongst whitewater aficionados – as the legends grew around rapids that had names like Lost Yak.

Historically, the river formed a natural boundary between north and central Chile, and was a frontier that the Spaniards were afraid to cross in their conquest of South America as the Auracarian (Mapuche) warriors on the southern side were extremely fierce and proud. From the Bío-Bío southwards, the land remained uncolonized until the late 1800s. But the momentum of commercial expansion finally brought Western-style farming and industry to the region.

A story of resistance and defeat was destined to be repeated in the 1980s. Sadly, the Bío-Bío represents a battle lost against dam-builders. A major environmental campaign failed to stop a series of six hydro constructions from going ahead, the first of which began in 1993 and was finished in 1995. Though the river is still rafted, and remains a drawcard with its crystal waters fed by the snow cover of the Andes, it is a shadow of its former self.

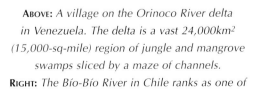

Above: *A village on the Orinoco River delta in Venezuela. The delta is a vast 24,000km² (15,000-sq-mile) region of jungle and mangrove swamps sliced by a maze of channels.*
Right: *The Bío-Bío River in Chile ranks as one of the top whitewater destinations of the world.*

and lucky to be alive. They forged on past Panama only to be accosted on the 'evil coast' of Colombia by drunken, or perhaps drugged, Indians.

Finally they made it to the relatively secluded Orinoco where it enters the Caribbean and Atlantic oceans via many channels. Their ordeal was far from over; they turned and paddled upstream, jumping in to haul the canoe bodily over rocks and sandbanks when the current became too strong. Light-headed and suffering from debilitating bouts of malaria, they had a close encounter with a deadly anaconda which only made off when Don Starkel waved his arms and roared like a grizzly bear. The pair reached the Casiquiare Canal, sustained by the knowledge that the rest would be downstream all the way to the coast on flowing, easy water.

When at last they cruised down the Amazon to gaze at the broad, muddy Atlantic stained to the horizon by the river water, they could only regret that their journey — which nobody before them had ever dreamed of doing, and probably will not attempt to repeat — was all over.

In 1977 a team of British whitewater kayakers under Mike Jones tackled the notorious Maipure, or 'Holy' Rapids, on the river some 1600km (1000 miles) from the sea in Venezuela. They encountered huge standing waves, giant whirlpools, and falls known as the Rapids of Death, and as word spread, their courageous antics drew large crowds of local boatmen and villagers to watch and wonder. The Maipure Rapids have barred entry to the Upper Orinoco by ocean-going vessels and even today portions of the river remain unexplored.

An important tributary of the Orinoco is the Caroni River. It also rises in the Guiana Highlands, and is celebrated for the Angel Falls, the world's highest, which plummet over an uninterrupted drop of 979m (3212ft) from the edge of the plateau of Auyán Tepuy, in Venezuela's Canaima National Park. Despite the name suggesting heavenly associations, the falls were in fact named after an American navigator, James Angel, who in 1935 became the first Westerner to see them.

LEFT: *Venezuela's Angel Falls, whose drop is recognized as the highest in the world.*
OPPOSITE: *A kayaker does an 'ender' on the Misahualli River in Ecuador, which cascades off the Andes and down to the rainforest lowlands of the Amazon basin.*

COLCA RIVER CANYON, PERU

Most rafting tour operators avoid the depths of the Colca canyon, objecting that it is for the certifiably insane only. Like the Tiger Leaping Gorge on the Yangtze in China, the Colca canyon, which passes through Aguada Blanca National Reserve in Peru, is popular mainly with hikers who are far safer taking in the perspective from above.

A nightmarish cleft on the Pacific side of the Andes range — the results of geological forces that are still thrusting the range higher at the edge of the Pacific rim, spawning volcanoes and earthquakes in the swirling mists — can be seen on the Colca River. To reach the river involves a scrambling descent of more than 2000m (6560ft). You can cross the Colca canyon and climb Mismi peak, from which Mike Horn (see p52) paraglided on his leap into the unknown. The canyon's route also passes through the villages of Chivay and Yanque, with their Spanish colonial churches set amongst Inca farming terraces.

The only creatures comfortable with the canyon's vertiginous altitudes are those born to them. Over this deep scar in the ribs of the Andes soars the rare and magnificent condor, a vulture and not an eagle, which happens to be the largest living bird with a wingspan of 3m (10ft). Voracious eaters, condors feed off carcasses but will attack living prey as large as deer. Being eaten by a condor, however, has been the least worry for a few intrepid parties of river-runners venturing into the canyon. A Polish group first penetrated the Colca in 1981 and returned in the 1990s for an expedition publicized in *National Geographic* magazine.

RIGHT: *On the Colca River, burros carry kayaks along the precipitous gorge to Hacienda Canco.*

Also in the 1990s, the American rafting pioneer Eric Hertz came to the Colca under the banner of his Earth River Expeditions, so setting the seal on the 'Colca Plunge' as the ultimate mission for those daring enough to take on the nastiest of rapids. At points, they found the river narrowed to just 3m (10ft) wide and was marked by undercut rocks and sudden leaps over numerous waterfalls higher than a house. The sight of bridal veil falls trailing in long wisps some 460m (1510ft) off the sheer rock walls lightened the mood, but not for long. At an average low-season flow of 11–22 cumecs (400–800cfs), the gradient and constrictions of the channel result in powerful jets of water belching with sounds like a freight train. Earth River went gingerly down the runnable sections and portaged their boats elsewhere, sometimes edge-on through narrow cracks in the wrenched and broken rocks.

Only Class 5 addicts need apply for trips on the Colca. But there will always be takers, and some will come back for more. To mark the 10th anniversary of their first descent of the Colca, the Polish team who pioneered the route invited American Joe Kane, of Amazon fame (see p51), along for the ride. Kane did not consider himself to be an extreme paddler but he was glad to be there, especially as some 'old hands' of the Amazon were on the trip. One was an expeditionary kayaker who had led on the tougher sections of the Apurimac, former British national whitewater team paddler Jerome Truran. This time Jerome was with his diminutive Canadian wife, Morna Fraser, who was up there with the best paddlers on the trip.

Morna was a competitive slalom kayaker with honours in national and international events, and had run some of the most challenging whitewater in British Columbia. She was impressed by the Colca but not fazed by it, and indeed on this occasion the river relented after a few hectic episodes. Only the low temperature in the canyon really bothered them.

A volcano had erupted, covering the sky with a thin cloud cover that made it distinctly cool in the deep belly of the Andes. Getting out to look at a Class 4 rapid, the chilled group discovered a small, filthy, smelly hot-spring, and promptly jumped in to carry on scouting from seats in the warm slime.

RIGHT: *A kayaker finely judges the drop on a series of falls known as the Seven Teacups, on the Río Claro in Chile.*

THE FUTALEUFU, CHILE

An environmental fight reminiscent of the Bío-Bío (see p57) is presently on to save a river fondly nicknamed the Fu. Further south than the Bío-Bío, nestled in a lush green valley and flanked by craggy forested mountains and glaciers, the Futaleufu River flows through the pristine landscape of Patagonia. This is an arid tableland stretching across Chile and Argentina, between the Andes and the Atlantic. Located roughly 240km (150 miles) southeast of the town of Puerto Montt in the Andes, the Fu is widely regarded as one of the most unspoilt, relatively safe, accessible, big-water rafting experiences in the world. Its breathtaking gorges offer over 30km (19 miles) of huge, crashing Class 4 and 5 whitewater. Río Futaleufu is similar to the Zambezi as a pool-and-drop river, but with a greater number and intensity of rapids.

The turquoise river was a popular choice for the 2000 Camel Whitewater Challenge Championships. The competition had taken place on the rock-infested Costa Rican rivers in 1998, and in the dramatic Augrabies gorge on the Orange River in South Africa in 1999. The paddlers had heard all about the Futaleufu and came prepared to do battle with big water, but soon realized that skilful navigation was essential too; it was both big and technical. They were confronted with huge holes, powerful surges off the cliff sides, and continuous standing wave sequences that left them shaking with nervous excitement.

Although large trout swim in the clear water and breathtaking snowcapped peaks surround the valley, the name Futaleufu simply means 'big river' in the local Mapuche dialect. This is reflected in the names of its rapids, of which many have Class 5 ratings: Khyber Pass and Himalaya, Inferno Canyon, the Terminator and

Throne Room. Zeta is the most spectacular, a Class 6+ rapid verging on the unrunnable even for top, daring boaters. Its Z-shaped flume (narrow channel) cuts into the granite cliffs, exposing a cave below where commercial rafting parties gather to camp after the compulsory walk. Rafts are floated along the shoreline attached to ropes.

In 1989, when Eric Hertz first visited the Fu, he knew it was the most beautiful river he had ever beheld. The hospitable local people welcomed the visitors, but warned them about the river because many regarded it as good only for drowning. They had no idea of its boating potential. The river valley had been largely uninhabited even up to the 1950s, except for Chilean cowboys (*huaso*) and a few hardy peasant communities.

Although a three-man group of kayakers had beaten Hertz to the river in 1985, he was the first to complete a full rafting descent of the Futaleufu. At first no-one wanted to believe there was a relatively warm river, in a stable, dry environment, only 1300km (800 miles) from Cape Horn, but gradually the idea caught on. Two years later Hertz and other operators established successful operations on the river, attracting tough, dunk-proof, paying clients to the gem of the southern Andes.

Apart from the Futaleufu, Hertz pioneered commercial rafting on other rivers such as the Colca, in Peru, with its deep canyon. He also introduced cutting-edge rafting trips in the Great Bend of the Yangtze River in China during the brief post-monsoon season when it is safe to run. Drawing on the technical expertise in rafting and rescue that had begun to accumulate in the late 1980s from international contacts and exchanges, Hertz began to use safety catarafts to accompany expeditions, installed footcups in paddleboats to provide a firmer seat for the crew, and offered a full training day for Class 5 rapids before setting off. Hertz's innovations were not unique but they were soundly integrated; without them, many rivers would have remained closed to all but the extreme rafters.

By the turn of the century, rafters on the Fu could experience a variety of exciting options, such as hiking or even horse-riding around the major rapids. Professional guides – who constitute a worldwide corps of professional rafters – now cater for people of all ages and experience in reasonably good physical condition. As the seasons change and the rains come of the snow

melts, these river guides move from the Himalayas to the Alps, then to Africa and Chile. Sadly, for their customers as much as for themselves and the local communities, another corps of internationalists also moves from river to river. These are the power companies and their financiers who build dams. The Futaleufu became a prime target of Chilean power companies in

the early 1990s. But this time something happened to delay or even stop the development.

Plans to dam the Futaleufu had been mooted at least since the Bío-Bío River in central Chile was earmarked for damming. But in 1995, Chile deregulated its electricity industry, allowing alternative modes of energy supply to be considered. A consortium of three US utility groups proposed to build enough natural gas lines from Argentina to cover most of Chile's electricity needs, which put damming of the Fu for hydro power on the back burner for the time being. The governor of the region announced his opposition to the dam and indicated that all efforts should be directed towards encouraging tourism.

ABOVE: *Symmetrical standing waves create a graceful surfing sport for a kayaker on Ecuador's Río Misahualli. As Andean rivers enter the Amazonian basin, the air temperature rises but the water remains cool for many miles yet.*

EUROPE, ASIA MINOR & MIDDLE EAST

PJÓRSÁ & JÖKULSÁ Á FJÖLLUM * SJOA * INN * MREZNICA * DOBRA * SOCA * JORDAN * DEZ

Europe's outdoor attractions include more than its share of skiing, hiking, mountaineering, and, of course, whitewater rafting and kayaking. Meltwater from the Alps feeds Lake Constance, the subcontinent's greatest natural reservoir, bordering on Germany, Switzerland and Austria. The lake lies on the course of one of its principal rivers, the Rhine, and is near to the sources of the other major waterways, the Rhône and Danube. All are wide and navigable, connected by canals to form lucrative trading routes between the Black Sea, the Baltic and the Mediterranean. Rapids and waterfalls occur in the mountain feeder streams.

But Europe's water riches extend much further, with great rivers in the Nordic countries of Iceland and Scandinavia, the UK, Italy, the Iberian Peninsula, Eastern Europe, and the Balkans. Further afield in Asia Minor and the Middle East are found the rivers of legend, religion and ancient civilizations, ranging from the Jordan (Israel) to the Euphrates (Turkey). Marking the border of Europe with Asia is the Volga, the longest river in Europe (and the 18th longest in the world), with 200 tributaries. It rises in the Valdai Hills near Latvia and flows for 3700km (2300

miles) to empty into the landlocked Caspian Sea, in southwest Russia. Disappointingly, it offers virtually no runnable whitewater as it is navigable by barges and ships for almost its entire length.

Climates and landscapes vary so radically across Europe, from glaciated fjordland to mellow Mediterranean valleys and stark biblical desert, that it is impossible to generalize about the rivers of this vast and complex region. Suffice to say that from the time of Eric the Red, Europeans using small boats have followed coastlines and rivers wherever they led, discovering new worlds as they did so. The great age of world discovery, from the Renaissance to the first half of the 20th century, brought forth generations of river explorers. Many were motivated by greed, by the lust for gold or the hunt for slaves; but some were saintly missionaries and others straightforward traders or loyal soldiers fighting for their royal masters. European river-runners have continued to be at the cutting edge of exploration today in South America, the Himalayas, and Africa. Their specialities are the smaller craft such as kayaks and river boards (hydrospeeds), along with the famous Klepper collapsible kayak.

ABOVE, LEFT TO RIGHT: *Norway's famous Ula Falls cascade between forested spurs in a series of drops sometimes run by kayakers; the Soca River winds through its valley in Slovenia, in the shadow of the Julian Alps; a kayaker descends the high-grade Nigardselva River in Norway.*
OPPOSITE: *The Chocolate Canyon on the Sjoa River, Norway, gets its name from the fact that rafting parties often stop for refreshments and candies in the gorge!*

NORDIC LANDS

THE PJÖRSÁ AND JÖKULSÁ Á FJÖLLUM, ICELAND

The very name Iceland might be enough to put off all but the hardiest boaters; yet, though this island in the North Atlantic has had its quota of bravehearted — even foolhardy — river adventurers, it also offers do-able whitewater trips to the average person who likes to stay reasonably warm and dry. Located just below the Arctic Circle and lulled by the remaining warmth of the Gulf Stream, Iceland lies on the mid-Atlantic Ridge and has been shaped by volcanoes and glaciers. The 'land of fire and ice' as Iceland styles itself, is so spectacular, so rich in birdlife, so pristine and culturally fascinating, that it deservedly belongs with the world's top river destinations.

Europe's largest ice sheet, Vatnajokull, lies to the southeast, covers about 8460 km² (3265 sq miles), and is larger than any body of ice in the Northern Hemisphere except for the Greenland ice sheet. Lava beds cover some 11 per cent of Iceland's land surface, which literally steams with geothermal springs, lava tubes, and bubbling mineral fields. The native vegetation consists of subarctic or arctic-alpine plants descended from those that survived the last ice age. Birch trees and willow grow in some places while the rest of the country is composed of barren mountains and deserts. Through all this rage springtime and summer rivers of unruly bulk with startlingly caramel-coloured water, some rivers being warmed by underlying lava beds. You can paddle

ABOVE AND RIGHT: *Stark cliffs rise (right) from the Jökulsá á Fjöllum in Iceland and a kayaker hits a wall of the river's freezing floodwater (above).*
FAR RIGHT: *A whitewater freestyle rodeo competitor.*

down a rollercoaster of spumy waves, passing eroding columns of basalt that threaten to topple into the flood (and sometimes do). The daring will leap from atop a column into the river below.

Iceland's storytellers have inherited the sagas, a prose narrative dating back to the early medieval era of Nordic and Celtic settlement which features historic legendary figures and events in the wild interior of the island — the so called Sprenqisandur ('exploding desert'), home of bandits, fairies and mythical creatures. This is not an area that Icelanders themselves wish to inhabit. More than half the population lives in or near Reykjavík, while others stay in villages and farms around the ocean fringes.

Rafting is a popular tourist attraction in Iceland, following in the wake of numerous explorations by leading boaters. In the three decades before the turn of the millennium, river explorers tackled Iceland's unpredictable waterways for the first time. By the end of the century they had still not exhausted all the possibilities.

The Pjórsá is Iceland's longest river, skirting the foot of Mount Hekla (1491m; 4892ft), the island's most famous volcano which last erupted in 1991. Adjacent to the impressive glacier Hofsjökull in the southeast of Iceland, the Pjórsá features stretches of medium- to high-grade whitewater with lots of action. There are

waterfalls on the river itself and in nearby ravines. One particularly impressive sight is the 122m (400ft) Háifoss ('high waterfall') in the Pjórsárdalur valley. It is said that in the past, heinous criminals would be thrown over waterfalls and could escape punishment if they survived the ordeal.

Waterfall-running has, however, attracted some of the world's best to Iceland. In 1996 Shaun Baker, eighttimes United Kingdom national rodeo whitewater kayak champion, made a freefall kayak attempt at the Aldeyjarfoss on the Skjálfandafljót River in central–north Iceland, where he succeeded in tackling the 19.7m (64ft) vertical drop of the falls in his kayak, claiming a new vertical drop world record (see panel on waterfall bids on p31).

A waterfall no-one is likely to run intentionally is the 44m (144ft) Dettifoss on the Jökulsá á Fjöllum. Probably Europe's widest and most powerful fall, the Dettifoss can swell to three times its normal volume in a matter of hours when warm summer conditions increase the glacial melt. In 1983 the Jökulsá á Fjöllum was the setting for one of the most imaginative and audacious kayak and raft trips ever undertaken. A pair of two-seater microlite aircraft, with kayaks for landing skis, was used in an assault on the 205km (128-mile) Jökulsá á Fjöllum from its source in a glacial cave to the sea in the Denmark Strait.

British research engineer Paul Vander-Molen conceived and carried out the plan to cross Iceland using kayaks and microlites. A 12-man team representing five nationalities — British, French, American, Australian and Icelandic team members — flew, boated and rappelled (abseiled) over treacherous icy badlands (characterized by eroded, sculpted landscape features) when a single slip could cost a life. The microlites scouted the river ahead and moved light loads of people and equipment across the terrain. Kayakers led by Paul's associate, Mick Coyne, a former Royal Marine, descended into a massive sinkhole in the ice, formed by steam from geothermal vents. Once down, they bathed naked in the mixture of boiling and freezing water in this ice chamber at the source of the Jökulsá á Fjöllum.

An award-winning 51-minute documentary was made for British Channel 4 TV named 'Iceland Breakthrough', and a book of the same name published. A tragic footnote to this risky and imaginative journey was that Paul Vander-Molen was tragically diagnosed with, and a few years later died from, leukaemia. His father Jack set up a leukaemia research and treatment foundation in his memory, to enable disabled adventurers to realize their 'outward bound' aspirations.

FREESTYLE COMPETITIONS AROUND THE WORLD

Rivers naturally attract festivals everywhere. Flea markets, story-telling jamborees that focus on river lore, traditional costume dancing and environmental gatherings are held wherever paddlers congregate to race or play in whitewater.

One of the most famous venues is at Rabioux, on the upper Durance River, near the town of Chateauroux in the hilly Hautes Alpes region of southeast France. A mythical standing wave on the Durance had attracted paddlers for three decades, until in the 1990s the development of 'river rodeo' (competitive stunt boating) made Rabioux a popular choice for championship events. A festival arose, with the organizers vowing that if the level of the Durance ever fell too low, they would sand-bag its banks to narrow the current and restore the wave.

The festival is carried off with Gaelic panache. Live television screens all over the site allow spectators to watch events and see action replays without crowding the riverbank. The finals at Rabioux are held at night under spotlights, with Heavy Metal and Grunge music booming out over the water. This is not everybody's notion of how to enjoy the ambience of a river, but the rodeo generation loves it.

Throughout the summer in North America, on rivers such as the Kern in California, the Gauley in West Virginia, and the Ottawa in Quebec, Canada, well-attended festivals feature a variety of water-based activities, including wet-wet-wet clown acts and downriver competitive rafting between regional or national teams. Paddlers show off their increasingly sophisticated moves in rodeo freestyle boating, which requires high levels of courage and co-ordination. Rodeo kayakers and rafting teams fling themselves into holes to see how many twists, vertical pop-ups and cartwheels they can manage in a minute or two.

In New Zealand, meanwhile, the closing year of the 20th century witnessed the World Rodeo Championships on the Fulljames (Ngaawaparua) Rapids on the Waikato River, near Taupo on the North Island. The hole in the rapids was wide and challenging, causing some intensely competitive spirits to ride it late into the night in order to learn its hydraulic habits. During breaks between events, jet-boats roared up the rapid packed with tourists. Sadly, during the events themselves, a young Irish woman paddler drowned in the turbulence below the Ngaawaparua Wave.

Ironically named Last Tanga in Parys, an annual rodeo championship in South Africa is held outside the town of Parys on the Vaal River, near Johannesburg, the economic hub of the country. The Afrikaans name of the hole here, Gatsien, can most politely be translated as 'see your rear end'.

THE SJOA, NORWAY

The Vikings, who originated from Scandinavia, created an entire culture around the skill of shipbuilding and the courage of their navigators. A millennium ago, these big, blond Norsemen sallied forth to attack and plunder Britain, simultaneously probing the North Atlantic to discover Iceland, Greenland and ultimately North America. Today their descendants, tamed by Christianity and loyal to the flags of Norway, Denmark and Sweden, are still great water lovers who to some extent have turned inwards to search out adventure on their inland waterways.

Norway, a country roughly the size of California but with only four million people, has wilderness on its doorstep virtually everywhere you go. Travellers rave about the crystal-clear rivers, the impossibly deep blue fjords, the brilliance of the landscape colouring, and the warmth of the welcome in this land which not long ago in geological time was covered by ice.

The Sjoa River (pronounced 'shew-ah') is the lair of the infamous Faukstad Hole – scene of many a rafting wipeout – as it comes roaring out of the glaciated Jotunheimen mountains of central Norway. In the vicinity of the Sjoa is the Ula, where daredevil kayaks sometimes race over a series of dramatic falls without much room for manoeuvre between the glistening rock faces. between the glistening rock faces. The Ula flows into the Lagen River which is later joined by the Sjoa, scene

PREVIOUS PAGES: The Sjoa River, Norway, combines magnificent forested scenery with fast, clear rapids.
OPPOSITE: Crewmen are sprung into the Sjoa River as a raft slams into the notorious Faukstad Hole – fast, steep, and culminating in a strongly recycling wave.

of the annual Sjoa Kayak Festival in mid-July. Situated in the southern province of Oppland, not far from Lillehammer, where the 1994 Winter Olympics were held, the Sjoa is regarded as the best accessible stretch of whitewater in Norway.

The first commercial trips offered on the Sjoa were put together in the early 1980s by Bill McGinnis, owner of the Californian company, White Water Voyages. Today the river sees about 20,000 rafters annually and an untold number of kayakers. It is split up into many different sections over its 90km (55-mile) course with everything from flat-water lakes to suicidal waterfalls and Class 6 unrunnables.

Rafting pro guide Anders Blomqvist, a Swede, reports that in 1993 he arrived to take up his job as head guide for a Sjoa company. The river had a reputation for being safe but extreme. In the first rapid, known as Gulf Stream, a Canadian guide mysteriously broke his leg and had to be bussed out. Too bad, thought Anders. From there he instructed all his guides to continue the trip down the middle of the river just to see if it was runnable at all – which they all did 'with confidence and a lot of screaming'. As usual, the rivergod had the final say and in the infamous Faukstad Hole, 200m (655ft) from the take-out, Anders' raft slammed into a monster foam pile that belonged more on the Zambezi River in Zimbabwe. It kept the team side-surfing for about five minutes, yelling with fear and exhilaration.

Undaunted, and not much the wiser, Anders floated with a party of 16 clients into the same hole the next day. In full view of a national television camera, he broke his nose, flipped the raft, and dumped the whole crew in the foaming waters; and worse was to come. Running upstream to get help, he saw that four rafts had capsized. In all, there were 32 swimmers in various states of desperation and unable to hear his shouting in the wild confusion. He got into his car and roared off like a Formula One driver to a local shop to call for helicopter assistance. This incident could have been the ultimate shame for him as a river guide; instead there were rewards. Finishing the day in front of the television with a few beers, the guide team got to watch themselves on the national news doing megaflips; the next day they made it onto the front pages of every newspaper. By the following weekend, bookings for this 'safe but extreme' river had increased sevenfold!

THE EUROPEAN ALPS

THE INN, AUSTRIA/SWITZERLAND

The romantic Tyrol region of Austria is an adventure centre for the whole of Europe, with hundreds of miles of hiking trails and many renowned ski-runs, rock climbs and mountain-biking challenges. Here, too, is found one of the most exciting whitewater rivers in Europe, the Inn. Rising near Saint Moritz in eastern Switzerland, the Inn crashes down steep gradients to flow generally northeast, forming the border between Germany and Austria before finally joining the Danube. Adjoining the Inn, the Ziller valley is the hub of activities focusing on rivers, including rafting and kayaking, with hydrospeed swimming and canyoning having been introduced more recently.

Alpine rivers follow deeply incised valleys, and so it is with the Inn. Between Landeck and Innsbruck in the western arm of Austria, the Inn flows through the Imst

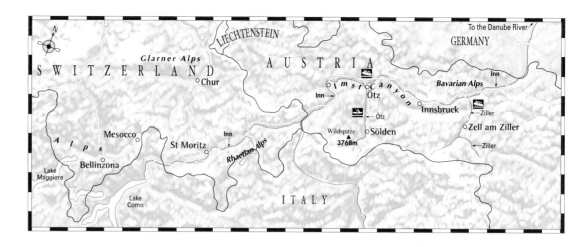

canyon, where the rapids are upfront and challenging. It is just near here that the annual Fasching festival is held, the legend being that this early spring ritual of pre-Christian origin rids the area of winter's cold and frost. But no-one should count on that. In the gorges of the Inn and its feeder rivers, sunlight penetrates for only a few hours a day and the water remains cold.

In 1969, the young British paddler Mike Jones (who would later become famous for running the Blue Nile of Ethiopia and Sudan, and kayaking down Everest) joined an expedition on a 130km (80-mile) stretch of the Inn which continental paddlers rated impossible. The British group were stunned by the precipitous rivers of the Alps, which seemed to fall over numberless rock hazards where a wrong move would pose serious dangers to life and limb. The Inn, confined by a steep-sided gorge, occupied them for five days and was without doubt the hardest piece of water anyone in the team had attempted; eight fibreglass kayaks were lost and one paddler, Trevor Eastwood, was nearly killed. Nevertheless, they finished the course, made a name for themselves, and opened up the river for the future.

Perspectives have changed since then: the river is boated continually from early spring to early winter, but it has lost none of its terrors for the unskilled. Meanwhile, entering the Imst gorge are tributaries of the Inn, the Ötz and Ziller, which have equally high-grade thrills for the truly audacious. Top-class guiding is available everywhere, though the more advanced Alpine river routes do require you to have previous rafting experience. The big plus is that at the end of the day, one is only minutes away from mellow ski lodges where wet and chilled bodies may be comforted with mulled wine beside a log fire.

PREVIOUS PAGES: *River-runners portage around the Urrum Fall on the Ula River, Norway.*
LEFT: *The furious spring meltwaters of the Ötz.*
RIGHT: *The Stubai Alps rise beyond the Inn River, which originates near St Moritz in Switzerland.*
FOLLOWING PAGES: *A view across the Inn River near Imst in Tyrol, with the Stubai Alps in the distance.*

THE REMARKABLE KLEPPER BOAT

The sport of kayaking got off to a colourful start in the 19th century thanks to a Scots devotee, John MacGregor. He spent part of his youth in Halifax, Nova Scotia, in Canada, where he probably saw the sealskin-and-whalebone kayaks used by the Inuit (Eskimo) peoples. Back in England he became a barrister-at-law in the Temple, London, but his true vocation was that of gentleman paddler. He designed and had constructed a heavy clinker-built, cedar and oak kayak called the Rob Roy. In successive versions of this much-publicized craft, he undertook a series of daring trips across Europe, the Middle East, Russia, North Africa, Canada and Siberia. His book A Thousand Miles in Rob Roy *(1866) became a best-seller.*

MacGregor created a rage for what came to be known as 'canoeing', although it is properly called kayaking. Amongst those who followed his lead was the novelist, Robert Louis Stevenson. His classic travel journal, An Inland Voyage *(1878), described a canoe trip through Belgium and northern France with Sir Walter Grindlay Simpson. The next step in European river-running was the invention of the German folding kayak, or faltboot, patented in 1907 by Johannes Klepper of Rosenheim. Kleppers immediately caught on as Europe's answer to the American birch bark canoe and hard-hulled river scow.*

Generations of Europeans first explored their own whitewater rivers, then spread across the globe, pioneering routes along coastlines, across oceans and lakes, and opening up rivers in remote regions.

Although cumbersome in appearance, the Klepper (single- or double-seater) is light, sturdy, flexible and portable, making it ideal for pack-and-go journeys. Originally comprising a framework of wooden rods with a canvas covering, Kleppers have undergone modern technical refinements but the design has changed very little over the years. Many imitations have appeared, generically known as Kleppers.

They have crossed the Atlantic Ocean, run Alpine rivers, forged routes across central Asia and high Himalayan lakes, and – with sails and outriggers – navigated the great lakes of North America and Central Africa. Most of this exploration has involved Europeans who simply love the boat.

The European kayaking tradition continues into the present. The craft of preference for high-grade rivers is now the plastic (polyethylene) kayak. Whitewater rivers in Scandinavia, Wales, Scotland, Corsica, the south of France, the Alps, the Pyrenees, and the Balkans contain some of the best technical runs anywhere; they tend to be short, steep, very wild and rocky – ideal for individual boaters but not usually appropriate for rafting crews. With the skills honed on their home rivers, European kayakers have penetrated mountain fastnesses in the Himalayas, Andes and Central Africa, bringing a certain élan to the sport.

THE BALKANS

THE MREZNICA, DOBRA AND SOCA, SLOVENIA AND CROATIA

For the last two decades, Balkan paddlers from two countries of the former Yugoslavian Republic, Slovenia and Croatia, have excelled in international rafting championships and kayak slalom. The secret of their success is in the rivers and culture of paddling that surrounds them.

Rivers like the Mreznica and the Dobra in the Dinaric mountain system (south of the eastern Alps) are accessible, clean and beautiful, demanding and well known to paddlers. In the days of communist rule, Eastern Europeans trained hard for Olympic canoeing events. Thereafter, the war that split Yugoslavia intervened to make paddling impossible for several years. More recently, whitewater rivers have returned to some sort of normality, which for river-runners means trying to preserve them for recreational use against the menaces of industrial growth and damming rather than having to avoid them altogether because of wartime bombardments and mine-laying. The experience of the war made Balkan river-runners even more determined to save, or restore, what they had.

Slovenia borders on Italy to the west, while to the north, the Julian Alps run along the spine that connects the country with Austria. In this mountainous region are many small-volume rivers that are steep, fast and clean. Conditions are ideal for one-day rafting tours and for sustained training throughout the warm summer, so it is not surprising that generations of Slovenian river guides have gone on to become world-class competitive paddlers.

LEFT: *Karst dykes (a build-up of calcium carbonate) across the Mreznica have created these waterfalls.*

Kayak and canoe slalom has been the preferred sport of the Slovenians, with rafting occupying a rather jocular second place. Slalom involves negotiating in minimum time between poles that hang over the water to create numbered 'gates'. The total of elapsed time plus the penalties for touching or missing a gate makes up the score, so the lowest score wins. The Soca River in Slovenia is a popular venue for these specialized events. Regarded as one of Europe's most picturesque rivers, the Soca runs through a national park in the northwest of the country, overlooked by Triglav peak. In particular, it is a drawcard for river-runners who dislike the mass-transit-in-rubber-buses atmosphere of rafting tours on Alpine rivers in more crowded parts of Europe. Unlike Croatia, Slovenia remained persistently peaceful throughout the 1990s, although the country also broke away from Yugoslavia.

Croatia shares Slovenia's south and east boundaries. The country's rivers have a peculiarity shared with parts of the Colorado and a few other rivers scattered over the world: instead of wearing down their channels, they build them up. Travertine – or layers of calcium carbonate deposited by the water – builds up into barriers that make sections of the rivers look like chains of lake interrupted by waterfalls. Known locally as 'karst', the substance is constantly adding to the height of the waterfalls and changing the rocks in the rapids.

Renowned Croatian riverman, Zeljko Kelemen introduced Dobra River rafting to United Nations troops working in a US hospital near Zagreb airport – the Dobra's 20km (12-mile) raftable stretch was not far away. That was in 1993, and the following year, hordes of locals asked Kelemen to organize more trips, forgetting that they were the ones who had expressed scepticism in the first place.

Another pioneer is Kelemen's Serb friend, Milka Smokjanovic, a widow with two grown children, who has put the Mreznica River on the rafting map. Visited by the American journalist Jon Bowermaster, Milka expressed her enthusiasm for ecotourism as she trudged around in multicoloured moon boots excitedly talking of rafting possibilities in the Balkans.

LEFT: *Kayaking over a small drop into a hole on the Soca River, Slovenia.*
FOLLOWING PAGES: *A kayaker in a modern playboat demonstrates cartwheeling on flat water on the Soca.*

MIDDLE EAST

THE JORDAN, ISRAEL

Rivers connect history with the future, and one river that has always taken mankind to new frontiers is the holy Jordan. It has drawn adventurers before our day, and, surprisingly, it has some whitewater that is rafted.

A section of the Jordan was paddled in 1869 by a British barrister named John MacGregor (see panel on page 80), the father of modern recreational canoeing, in his wooden kayak *Rob Roy*. At one point he was attacked by a mob who drove him into the shallows. They picked him up, boat and all, and deposited him in the tent of a local sheikh who did not quite know what to do with him. A true Victorian, MacGregor doffed his pith helmet at the sheikh and proceeded to read *The Times*, while his interpreters wheedled and bribed their way out of the situation. MacGregor did not complete the Jordan but carried on overland to the Red Sea, paddling a bit of that, too.

A million years ago, a major earthquake created the Syrian-African Rift which includes the Jordan valley, the Red Sea and the Rift Valley of Africa. The Dead Sea sank deep into the Jordan valley and was deprived of its natural outflow to the sea. Today, the Dead Sea is the lowest point on earth. Two-thirds of the water reaching it comes from the Jordan River, which empties into its northern end. Until the 1930s, the inflow of fresh water equalled the rate of evaporation, but national water projects on both sides have curtailed the flow drastically, to less than a quarter of what it was. Upstream, though, above Galilee, it is still a fairly strongly flowing river.

ABOVE: *The Jordan River, Israel.*
RIGHT: *The Coruh River in Turkey.*

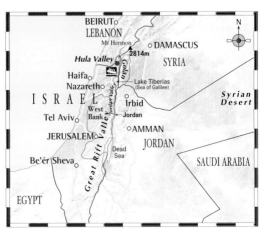

THE CORUH, TURKEY

The kinds of extended rafting trips in natural surroundings so popular in the Americas, Asia and Africa simply don't happen in Europe – unless you go to the fringes. A world of rafting possibilities opens up in Asia Minor and the Middle East.

Turkey's magnificent Coruh River originates in the Pontic mountains to follow a fast-flowing course to the Black Sea in Georgia. Small towns and villages located along the river bespeak the civilization of Turks going back to at least the 11th century, with the area as a whole representing a synthesis of the cultures of Eastern Anatolia and Georgia – Anatolia now contains three million Kurds. Colonies of red kites, which are threatened with extinction, still live among the rocks by the riverside, as do grey bears and mountain goats with distinctively hooked horns.

The Coruh River is frequented by sportsmen who come each year to raft, kayak and trek in the Kackar mountains of northeast Turkey. One of them is expert British kayaker Dave Manby, who first ran it in 1982 and loved it so much he returns again and again to run trips on a 120km (75-mile) stretch of Class 3–5 rapids.

The whole history of this region is closely bound up with its rivers and with memories of The Flood of the Old Testament. Mount Ararat, where Noah made his legendary landfall, lies 200km (125 miles) east of the Coruh. Further to the southeast are the Tigris and Euphrates rivers, running southwards. Once cradles of Western civilization, they are now the hub of potential conflict over water between Turkey, Syria, Iraq and Iran.

The most hallowed of the Jordan's sources is the spring of Baniyas, on the border between Israel and Syria. Here the Jordan rushes from the mountainside, fed by ground water deriving from the snows of Mount Hermon in Syria, to the northeast. It is here that the disciple Peter acknowledged Jesus as the Messiah. The river plunges over a waterfall into a cool, shady grotto, and then slows to soak into the fertile Hula valley.

Although the upper Jordan borders the disputed Golan Heights to the extreme northeast of the country, one of the world's most politically tense terrains, this does not stop crowds of pleasure-seekers from rafting and tubing along on the smooth, though swift, currents of the river. Below the retaining dams and pumping schemes of the Hula valley, the Jordan enters a series of gorges, descending a staircase of rapids with a considerable gradient. Here rafting operators have in the past offered trips culminating near the Jordan's entry into the Sea of Galilee.

In the centre of the country, between Galilee and the Dead Sea, the Jordan flanks the Palestinian West Bank and marks the border with the Kingdom of Jordan. This is certainly among the world's dangerous places. Israelis and Palestinians rub shoulders nervously as partitioning of the land proceeds, while Israeli and Jordanian troops face each other over the river along the peace treaty line of 1994.

It was not always so. In 1848 Lieutenant William F Lynch of the US Navy led a crew of 10 'young, muscular, native-born Americans of sober habits' down the river carrying carbines, a blunderbuss and bowie knives to frighten any marauding Bedouin. They had dragged two metal lifeboats by camel over almost impassable mountain trails to launch them on the Sea of Galilee. Under the command of Midshipman R Aulick, one of the boats, the

near the end. The 'Jordan goes mad', as Whiting put it, 'tumbling down and down, hitting large rocks and spurting upward, or twisting and turning between boulders in a white-foam rage'. By day nine, the river seemed to be flattening out as it approached the Allenby Bridge, a relic of the World War 1 Allied campaign for Palestine. Then Whiting paddled incautiously into a rapid that leapt at them with a 'mighty roar'. His canoe capsized, and it was luck or grace alone that let he and his companion escape from the deadly clutches of submerged trees in time to warn the others.

The austere lower Jordan could conceivably be a world whitewater destination with great spiritual appeal. But, lack of water and an unstable political situation make that impossible.

THE DEZ, IRAN

Dave Manby knew there must be many more rivers worth rafting in Asia Minor and the Middle East, but war and instability kept tourists away. After 20 years of enjoying the Coruh, he decided to dip his toes into the waters of Iran, which adjoins Turkey. On the strength of a few glimpses of the Dez River between railway tunnels in the Zagros mountains of Iran's Loristan province, Manby and a party of friends arrived in the year 2000 to run the river. It proved to be every bit as good as appearances had suggested; a gold strike amongst rivers.

The Zagros region is very large, comprising heavily eroded mountain ranges surrounding Iran's high interior basin and covering 10 provinces which contain nearly 60 per cent of the population of Iran. Most rivers of the country rise in the Zagros, including the Dez, which proceeds from the highlands to the plains of southern Iran and thence to the Persian Gulf. On this river one may still see traditional platform rafts, supported by floating skins or drums; they are used for trade. One picturesque application of the rafts is to convey local holidaymakers across the Dez to the shelter of cool caves that have been hollowed out of the cliffs at water level.

The Dez is not entirely unknown in the world at large as it has made news in recent decades. Before the Iranian Revolution, Shah Pahlavi dammed the Dez above the city of Dezful, ignoring international protests and saying that the natural and climatic conditions of Iran did not allow the country to waste even one drop of water; but he neglected to mention that by restricting rainy season flows,

the dam could drastically impact on the livelihoods of peasants in the fertile plain of Jolgeh-ye Khuzestan near the Persian Gulf. The Shah named the dam after himself but it may well have contributed to his downfall, and after the revolution it was simply called the Dez Dam.

The river was in the headlines again during the ghastly Iran-Iraq war when the railway bridge over the river, at Telle Zange, was bombed by Saddam Hussein, reputedly delaying the war's end by about three years. The untended wreckage of this bridge marked the pull-out spot for Manby's expedition. The team of three kayakers — Manby, Guy Baker and Bob Merchant — had succeeded in running the Dez from near DoRud to Telle Zange, a first descent that held many nervous moments. Following a narrow valley with Class 3–4 rapids, the river entered dramatic gorges, prompting comparisons with the Grand Canyon. With great trepidation the team manoeuvred round corners where cliffs rose 300m (1000ft) straight out of the water, fully aware that their way might be blocked by an unrunnable rapid with no way out or back. After the junction with the Sezar River, the volume of water more than doubled and the team leapfrogged down eddies, curbing their eagerness to rush on down the river as ever more spectacular vistas unfolded on each bend. Finally they found a route through the last major rapid, and hauled their kayaks up the bank in 40°C (110°F) heat.

Memories of the Iran-Iraq war may not have faded, but the group of kayakers were bowled over by the incredible hospitality of the Iranian people. The party, grinning from ear to ear, was openly welcomed into Iranian homes and allowed to sleep in the police station. They have since vowed to return, in force.

Fanny Skinner, rode out the battering of some 176 rapids to reach the Dead Sea. Lynch produced superb maps with bathymetric markings confirming that the Dead Sea was the lowest place on earth.

Shortly before World War II, a group using Klepper folding kayaks paddled the same route down the Jordan River, through the desert of Judea. A Middle East specialist writer for *National Geographic* magazine, John D Whiting, led a four-man expedition through the Jordan's sweltering flood plain, the Zor. Although the river winds interminably, it is steep, and the party nearly came to grief

LEFT: *Kayakers drop into a trench on the Dez River.*

ASIA, SIBERIA & CHINA

KATUN & CHUYA * CHATKAL AND PSKEM * YANGTZE

Tens of thousands of rivers spill from the mountain ranges all around central Asia, including those of Siberia, Tibet and China. The Ob, Lena, Yangtze (Chang Jiang), Tsangpo (Brahamaputra) and Indus all have their birthplace in the tangle of geological upheavals that has created the world's highest peaks. It is almost impossible to imagine the river-running opportunities in this vast region all at once — the character of the rivers is so varied and the abundance of whitewater so magnificent. Hundreds of languages are spoken in this region, and lifestyles vary from the survivalism of nomads inhabiting windswept plains to the spiritual asceticism of Tibetan monks chanting their mantras in hilltop temples.

It is estimated there are well over 100,000 rivers in Siberia alone, many of them frozen in winter, and when the ice melts, most of the flow heads northward across a vast lowland plain to the Arctic Ocean. Though the rivers of the plains are slow-flowing and wide, at their many-forked origins they are steep and strong. The continent is dominated and ringed by mountains still largely in the process of formation, with tectonic forces thrusting from the south and volcanic activity breaking the crust in the far northeast. Southwest of Siberia, the Mongolian mountain massif formed by the Altai and Tien Shan ranges scythe around to join the Pamirs (Tajikistan), the Hindu Kush (Afghanistan and Pakistan) and the Himalayas (India and Nepal). The world's mightiest ranges, they all contain peaks well over 7000m (23,000ft), from whose flanks rivers pour in profusion.

Modern river-runners can scarcely catch their breath in the mad pursuit of new rivers to run and rumoured explorations to join. To include all of central Asia's raftable rivers would take a huge compendium on its own; instead we follow the saga of recent journeys of discovery by the Russians and Chinese themselves, along with Americans, Europeans, Australians and New Zealanders.

Little infrastructure exists; some that there was has deteriorated and crime is a problem. Officialdom is an obstacle (especially in China), but away from roads and rubber stamps, the people are extremely welcoming. The scars of industrialization mar some areas around the cities, but elsewhere the land and the waterways have shown remarkable powers of regeneration, or rather obliteration driven by blizzards and ever-encroaching forests and deserts.

ABOVE, LEFT TO RIGHT: *The Gilgit River skirts the Hindu Kush and Karakoram mountains of Pakistan; a narrow, rickety bridge crosses the Pskem River in Uzbekistan; the upper Yangtze River meanders across the vast Tibetan Plateau.*
OPPOSITE: *Giant slabs of ice calve off the Ferchenkar Glacier on Communism Peak (7495m; 24,584ft) as kayakers begin a descent of the Stormy River. The trip shown here took place in 1989 before the Soviet Union collapsed. The glacier is the largest in the Soviet Union.*

RIVERS OF SIBERIA

Siberia, whose boundaries are the Arctic and Pacific oceans to the north and east, China and Mongolia to the south, and Kazakhstan and the Urals to the west, is no longer an administrative region but is part of greater Russia. This factor has induced local paddlers to treat the Siberian hinterland as their own and take possession of it in the name of the rivergods. They have not confined themselves to Siberia but have pioneered rivers in Russia's other mountain ranges, including those in the European regions — Karelia and the Kola Peninsula flanking Finland in the northwest; the Carpathian mountains in the Ukraine (a former Russian Republic) in the west; the Caucasus mountains to the southwest; and the Urals bordering on the great Siberian Plain.

For epic grandeur, nothing beats the Siberian rivers and those of the republics of Kazakhstan, Kyrgyzstan, Uzbekistan and Tajikistan lying to the southwest. Whitewater comes thundering out of the rumpled heights of the Sayan and Altai mountains in southern Siberia, the Tien Shan (to the southeast) and the lofty Pamirs beyond. The desolate tableland of the Pamirs plateau in Tajikistan, averaging 4000m (13,000ft), is inhabited by dour, fur-clad nomads who tend to regard visitors as another species and therefore to be shunned.

By contrast, the people of western Siberia are friendly and colourful, and their surrounding mountains extremely well-watered. The Sayan and Altai, forming the barrier between Russia and Mongolia, have heavy precipitation, mainly in summer and autumn. Along the Katun ridge of the Altai, up to 2000mm (80in) is recorded annually. Seasonal snowfalls from the buran or purga winds streaking out of the Arctic can average 3m (10ft), with the result that the rivers are fed by dozens of glaciers. Except in the buzzing heat of midsummer,

the climate is harsh, cold and wet. To the east lies the Chuyskaya steppe, where the temperature in midwinter can plummet from an average -32° to -62°C (about -20° to -70°F) in cold snaps.

Not surprisingly, when the whitewater boating craze took off in the Soviet Union during the 1970s and 1980s, the great water and short hot Siberian summer began to draw Russian rafters to the scene. Although the name Siberia is almost synonymous with suffering due to its association with the Soviet Gulag, and the tradition of Tsarist banishments before that, it took on a new dimension as Russian rafters, inured to the cold and ready for any ordeal by water, attacked the Siberian rivers with a mixture of rough courage, vodka, and improvised equipment.

THE KATUN, ALTAI MOUNTAINS

The Katun River originates in one of the wildest and most sparsely populated spots on the planet: at the borders of Russia, Kazakhstan, China, and Mongolia, in the Altai mountains, about 4000km (2500 miles) southeast of Moscow. The long isolation of the Soviet Union from the West, combined with the rough climate, have ensured that only few outside Siberia have been able to experience the river's strength and its surrounding beauty. The Katun starts from a glacier on Belukha peak, the highest point of Siberia and the Russian Far East at 4506m (14,784ft), and soon joins the Biya River to give birth to the powerful Ob. The Irtysh-Ob is the longest river in Siberia and the fifth longest in the world, at 5570km (3460 miles).

The upper Katun is an inaccessible damp cellar staircase of continuous cascading rapids for 'hairball boaters' only. The river makes a half-circle around Mt Belukha, with alpine meadows separating the snow-

line and the rich forests of firs, larch and cedar. The middle Katun is a substantial river on which rafting trips of up to 10 days are conducted. Other sections of the river are truly wild and considered unrunnable even by addicts prepared to take a risk.

No doubt the time could come for the worst sections to be bested by paddlers, but it has not happened to date — for over a decade, the Russian government has been threatening to build a hydroelectric dam that will interrupt the flow of the Katun, consequently destroying its whitewater attractions.

RUSSIANS TACKLE THE CHUYA

A tributary of the Katun, the Chuya, seeps out of the camel-breeding area of mountain steppe called Kosh-Agacha. As it gathers speed and volume, it tumbles through the Mazhoy Cascade, an 8km (5-mile) canyon with vertical walls and stepped Grade 6 rapids such as the feared Praesidium. In summer, the valley is sunny and dry, though the river itself carries yellow-grey meltwater heavy with glacial grit and sediments from the fast-eroding Altai. At a low level of around 40 cumecs (1400cfs), it offers a challenging Grade 4–5 run. At any level above 85 cumecs (3000cfs), Mazhoy could be the last run for inexpert paddlers, with rapids such as Hippo (Begemot), Turbine, and Tourclub 'Horizon' lurking in wait.

The Chuya had been attracting rafting fans for three decades, but it was only in 1989 that it suddenly made its presence known to international rafters. A number of American, British, European, Australian, and Costa Rican paddlers responded to the invitation of the Soviet Peace Fund to compete in the 10th annual Chuya Rally, a raft slalom competition. The rally had been held since 1979 on a purely domestic basis, with the number of participants having grown from 18 to 88 representing 22 Soviet cities.

When Russian river-runners began to make contact with the outside world, they amazed their foreign counterparts with a cowboy attitude that would put the Wild West to shame. A seasoned American rafting guide, Doc Loomis, expressed the astonishment of the Westerners at the Russian turnout and the nature of their equipment. Oars and paddles were cut from trees, and one innovative paddler had even made a life jacket from a whole airline seat that he wrapped around himself. In an interview with fellow-American rafting writer, Jeff Bennett, Loomis described the ingenuity of the Russian-made craft named *plohts* (platforms floating on bulbous inflated chambers) and catarafts:

'Every boat was constructed different, constructed with whatever timbers, tubing, twine, or bags they could get their hands on. Most of the tubes were giant bags that held plastic bags full of air.'

But the apparent crudity at that time masked great technical sophistication, and the Russians demonstrated formidable rafting skills. Their craft, made from industrial scrap, hard aluminium tanks and discarded para-chutes, amongst other detritus of the Soviet state, were marvels of design innovation. Local boat crews outmanoeuvred their international rivals, and everyone who saw the newfangled boats in action was impressed. Designs ranged from four-person paddlecats — boats with twin hulls crewed by paddlers rather than skippered by an oarsman — to the weird *plohts* and zany innertube *bubliks* (two enormous tractor tubes standing upright and joined by planks). The Russian concepts were certainly innovative and they promoted a new surge in whitewater inventiveness. It was not long before Russian-style rafts began to appear in the USA.

Russian methods of river rescue held more surprises. Fearless rescuers, wearing harnesses tied to long pieces of rope, simply flung themselves into the rapids to grab swimmers and lay hold of capsized boats. Loomis described the rescuers — called *zhivets* (referring to the live bait used by fishermen to catch bigger fish) — as 'human throw ropes'. These heroics have since been adopted elsewhere; swimmer rescue is most practical where someone in the water is grabbed before drop-ping over a fall or being swept into a logjam. Russian rafting has become somewhat more refined since those days. The equipment is no longer scrap and is professionally made, and Russians have piloted their paddlecats down American rivers to demonstrate their viability, yet the rambunctious spirit attributed to the Russian bear remains undiminished.

Regrettably, in Russia itself crime has been on the uptake. River-runners seeking access to rivers and official information about them find there is bribery and theft as police share a 'common pocket' with officials who extort bribes from visitors. By way of warning, 'necessary notes about unpleasant things' are offered to intending visitors by Vladimir Gavrilov, a prominent paddler now based in the USA, who is involved in a project code-named RAFT, which brings Russian and US paddlers together.

OPPOSITE: *In summer, the Chuya's muddy melt-waters ripple through green conifer-lined banks.*
ABOVE: *The rugged landscape of the Altai mountains, Siberia, seen across a flat section of the Katun River.*

BAIKAL – A LAKE RENEWED

Lake Baikal lies on the borderline of the Siberian platform, which is framed by a belt of folded mountains where tectonic movements of the earth's crust are taking place. In 1862 about 200km² (77 sq miles) of lakeside land sank under water to a depth of several metres as the result of a prodigious earthquake. To this day the entire region is unstable, with about 2000 tremors a year being measured.

Baikal is known as the Pearl of Siberia and is a designated World Heritage Site for its incredible diversity of wildlife and scenery. It is the largest body of fresh water in Eurasia, equalling Belgium in extent; it is also Earth's oldest lake (25 million years) and its deepest at 1620m (5315ft).

In central Siberia, rafting developed all around the city of Irkutsk, situated near the shores of Lake Baikal. Here the Angara River flows out to join the Yenisey on its way north to the Arctic Ocean. Keeping the lake topped up are some 336 rivers and streams including the Barguzun, Selenga, Khara-Murin, and Snezhnaya, the latter being a popular whitewater run.

At the time of the Chuya Rally in 1989, the Soviet Union was undergoing massive political change as glasnost began to prise open a window on the world. Soviet planners paid little or no attention to the recreational needs of ordinary people, and even though international tourism was recognized as a source of useful foreign exchange, no attempt was made to promote ecotourism in the far-flung states of the USSR. Rafters in Russia coined the slogan 'Rafting to freedom', which was then used as a promotional technique by operators named Team Gorky. Rafters sought a new kind of personal challenge over which the bureaucrats had little say. Adventure had put them in touch with individualist values.

Remote as it is, Baikal has been affected by industrialism and pollution, while some of the rivers have been cluttered by extensive logging. In Soviet times, the Baikalsk Pulp and Paper Plant became a focal point of a growing environmental lobby led by the world-renowned dissident Andrei Sakharov, a leading nuclear physicist regarded as the father of the H-Bomb in Russia, and supported by many river-runners. Being very outspoken, Sakharov was exiled to the provincial city of Gorky, but he could not be silenced and eventually his criticisms won popular support.

In the 1960s, environmentalists lost the battle to stop construction of the pulp factory. But victory of a kind came when, after the disintegration of the Soviet Union, a law was passed to protect the lake and rivers. Though the pulp mill is still there, and of concern to UNESCO which granted Baikal its World Heritage status, there is hope for the future. The region is open for tourism and much of its unhappy, grimy history is being overcome by determined efforts to renew the gloss on the pearl.

THE CHATKAL AND PSKEM, KYRGYZSTAN

The rivers of the Tien Shan, the mountain range separating Kyrgyzstan and northwest China, cross the ancient Silk Road which once joined the cities of Bukhara, Samarkand and Tashkent in neighbouring Uzbekistan. For millennia, raw silk was exported on this route from China. The smuggling of silkworm eggs was punishable by death. In 1966, Tashkent, capital of the Uzbek republic, was heavily damaged by an earthquake, tragically illustrating something that geologists had suspected for a long time.

Although the name Tien Shan means 'celestial mountains', they are hardly at peace within themselves for they lie at the centre of a belt of violently deformed features on the earth's surface. From the Pamirs to the southwest, north across the Tien Shan to the Altai, Asia's tectonic compression curls like a whiplash across the face of the land. The powerful upward displacement of the earth's crust, or orogenic belt, of Central Asia is one of the most spectacular examples of active deformation within a continental interior, accommodating as much as 40 per cent of the modern-day shortening, or continental compression, between India and Siberia.

To go whitewater boating in Russia you fly thousands of miles across trackless steppe, or maybe catch a train, then leap onto a rickety truck, transfer to an animal-drawn cart, and get off to hike down a muddy track through bear country. Finally when you reach the river, you build your raft. Inflatable bladders are glued and stitched together, birch or pine trees cut and roped-up to make frames. When the process is concluded, some rafters knock back Coke Po Ruski — a dark mixture of instant coffee powder, sugar, and vodka — and jump onto the freezing river wearing hockey helmets and used woollen sports clothing, as wetsuits are in short supply. At night the locals love to wage philosophical conversations for hours at a time, swallowing gallons of strong black tea sometimes laced with something stronger. Vodka, remarked one participant, is the 'national decease' of Russian river-runners.

A FIRST DESCENT OF THE CHATKAL

In 1993, Anglo-Irish kayaker Liam Guilar was one of a party of four who travelled to the Tien Shan to paddle its rivers. A literature teacher in Australia, Guilar wrote about his Russian trip in a website book, *Dancing with the Bear*. Initially the foreign rafters were suspicious of anyone who drifted into their camp, but after a few weeks they relaxed and learnt to enjoy the company of Russians.

Theirs was to be the first kayak descent of the turbulent Chatkal and tightly confined Pskem rivers, although the rivers had been rafted since the mid-1970s. They are tributaries of the Syr Darya River which flows into the landlocked Aral Sea (embraced by Kazakhstan and Uzbekistan) off to the west.

The group ascended the 3500m (11,400ft) Black Camel pass on a switchback road, crossing a rickety wooden bridge that threatened to collapse under the weight of their truck. (The first law of river-running is: the worse the road, the better the trip.)

After passing camps of wild-looking men and memorials to those who had not made it up the road, the group finally stood next to a turquoise river, the Sandalash, on which they boated down to the Chatkal. Liam Guilar found the landscape of ravaged peaks, the rain-softened air, the evenings smelling of damp hay, and the roaring river, so overwhelming that he felt 'an absurd, irrepressible, inescapable sense of joy'.

The Chatkal was a river made in heaven. Fifty-one rapids were graded 3 and above, and as Guilar and his team went along, they casually named them — Binary Proposition (life or death) and All Day's Sucker (it went on for miles) were among these.

The action kept coming; there was nowhere on the five-day Chatkal trip that anyone had to paddle to keep moving. The river moved swiftly through gorges that were 'neck-wreckingly beautiful', its water green and very cold. When the party got off the river to wander along a path to a ruined village, Guilar felt he was back on the Salmon River in faraway Idaho: he was experiencing the same warm dry air, same smells, same river noise. He marvelled at how the Kyrgyzsian peasants had broken their backs to plant gardens in countryside almost biblical in its simplicity, only to see their children leave and the place return to wilderness as they grew older and died.

On the Pskem, after days of tight manoeuvring, Guilar and a friend tried their hand on a Russian paddlecat. They knelt in the two bow positions with two paddlers behind, their knees gripped by metal hoops. In Guilar's own words:

'In the bow you feel you're being hurled at rocks, dropped into holes from a great height, buried in the frothing water. Breathless and heaving on the flexing paddle, the barge responded painfully slowly. We made a good run. And suddenly I realized how much skill the Russians possessed to be able to run this technical water.'

Differences in national character emerged right from the start. The visitors paddled kayaks alone; the Russians made communion with each other in team paddlecats. The visitors liked to sit up late savouring the atmosphere around the campfire, while these Russian river guides would vanish to snore in their tents. It wasn't long, however, before the Westerners taught them to stay up late and the Russians in turn taught them how to drink huge quantities of vodka without a hangover. By the end of the trip, language barriers aside, the walls had broken down.

'When you see the evil stuff the Russians have run in their homemade craft, you realize what hardcore boating really is,' Guilar recalled later. 'They would tell us stories of walking for ten days over the mountains, carrying enough gear for an extended river trip, and we'd feel absurdly guilty that we could just drive to a put-in, paddle for a day and go home.'

The international subculture of river-running increasingly binds adventurers from many backgrounds and walks of life.

Opposite: *Lake Baikal in Siberia, which has been declared a World Heritage Site, holds so much water that it has been calculated it would take an entire year to fill the lake if all the world's rivers flowed into it together.*

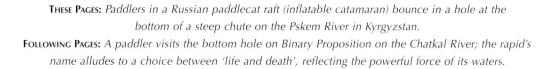

THESE PAGES: *Paddlers in a Russian paddlecat raft (inflatable catamaran) bounce in a hole at the bottom of a steep chute on the Pskem River in Kyrgyzstan.*

FOLLOWING PAGES: *A paddler visits the bottom hole on Binary Proposition on the Chatkal River; the rapid's name alludes to a choice between 'life and death', reflecting the powerful force of its waters.*

RIVERS OF CHINA

During the insane and tortured years of Chairman Mao Ze Dong's Cultural Revolution, from 1967 till about 1975, the youth of China were exhorted to flow 'like a red river that sweeps away the exploited classes'. China, containing one-quarter of mankind, hardly needed a human-inspired catastrophe to add to the misery already wrought by its prodigious rivers. Inured as they are to great leaps backwards — misfortunes caused by natural disasters and political events, themselves a product of ecological pressures on the land — the Chinese have developed great respect for their rivers. It was only to be expected that when Americans announced the first bid to raft the Yangtze River from source to sea, Chinese adventurers would impulsively jump in before them. The resulting rivalry kept the Chinese public riveted to their TV screens and newssheets, arousing major national interest in the exploits of whitewater warriors. Everyone with a hankering to prove themselves started making plans to conquer China's unknown and unrun rapids. An unfortunate byproduct of the craze was that the communist bureaucracy was able to capitalize on the national sentiment that the rivers belonged to the people and not to foreigners wearing reflective sunglasses to hide their 'round eyes'. As a result, permits are hard to come by, expensive, and can be maddeningly time-consuming to obtain.

The rivers of China (and its neighbouring state, Mongolia) have scarcely been touched but for certain sections of the Yangtze (Chang Jiang), Salween and Tsangpo, where Chinese teams have gone and Westerners have sometimes been permitted to go. Much more awaits exploring. China's second longest river, the Huang, or Yellow (which gets its name from the yellow silt it carries), flows through a series of deep gorges in the Gobi and Ordos deserts — but there is no record of any first descent from source to sea.

LEFT: *Upper Gorge, Yangtze River, China.*
ABOVE: *Jade Dragon Snow Mountain, Yangtze.*

THE YANGTZE (CHANG JIANG)

The Yangtze – known to the Chinese as Chang Jiang, or 'long river' – is Asia's longest waterway and the world's third longest. From its headwaters in the Kunlun Mountains in the southwest section of Qinghai Province, it flows generally south along the edge of the Plateau of Tibet. In all, it is 6300km (3900 miles) long and falls 4900m (16,100ft) before emptying into the sea in an extraordinarily long, flat estuary near Shanghai. For more than 2000 years, the lower half of its course has been a commercial highway through the earth's most crowded country.

Until nearly two decades ago, no-one had attempted to boat the upper half of the Yangtze where the river was considered to be an impassable torrent, a raging dragon churning and twisting through a series of canyons. Suddenly, in the 1980s, several groups appeared on the water, determined to ride 'the dragon's back'. A slight liberalization of Chinese policy towards its own sports participants and towards foreign visitors allowed these challengers to come forward with their inflatable rafts and media releases. In no time, a race developed between two groups of Americans and two Chinese, all intensely competitive and none very willing to share techniques or publicity with the others. The full story is told in US writer Richard Bang's wonderful book, *Riding the Dragon's Back*, which is as much a narrative of courage and tragedy as a study in the group dynamics of action and reaction under extreme stress.

In 1986, the spirit of competition was spurred by the tragic example of a 32-year-old photographer from Sichuan, Yao Maoshu. While still a student, Yao had decided to run the entire length of the Yangtze in a raft – alone. His plan was to float from the river's source at Mount Geladandong to Shanghai. Energized by reports that an American expedition led by Ken Warren was planning a similar trip, Yao kissed his wife goodbye, and by bus and finally yak caravan, crossed the great wastes to the glacier at the foot of Mount Geladandong.

His small inflatable, the *Dragon's Descendant*, carried him 970km (600 miles) before he reached the constricted, dramatic Tongtian Gorge. Somewhere among the 17 visible drops in the short canyon, Yao's raft, newly laden with donated food and a shotgun to drive off bears, flipped. His lifeless body was spotted half a day downstream. Yangtze rafting had its first national hero. Soon afterwards Ken Warren, an experienced rafter from Tualatin, Oregon, arrived with an ABC-TV crew under producer John Wilcox to make an insert for the programme 'The American Sportsman'.

The race was on. Two Chinese expeditions were independently launched, one by the sports and scientific agencies of the Chinese government, and another by a group of friends from Luoyang in Sichuan Province. They set out to conquer the river before any Westerners could do so. After much bickering and official interference, the two expeditions joined forces and a handful made it to the coast to complete the entire journey in over five

months: eleven survived after rafting much, though not all, of the Yangtze's length. In the meanwhile, Warren's expedition had been abandoned for some five weeks, roughly 1600km (1000 miles) from its starting point at the source, after the leader himself walked out on his followers. Overall, the toll in human lives was high. Ken Warren lost the photogapher, David Shippee, as a result of altitude sickness leading to pneumonia, while half of the members of the Chinese groups drowned.

During the course of the Chinese expedition, their most extraordinary moments came in the frightening rapids of Tiger Leaping Gorge in Yunnan Province, bordering on Sichuan. Three courageous rafters ran the Hutiao Shoal by sealing themselves inside a sandwich made of two inflatable rafts. The river here squeezes between near-vertical gorge sides and plunges down twin channels that separate around a pyramid of black rock. Two were killed, the third rescued from a ledge after three days. Two more rafters put in below the Hutiao Shoal in a similar sealed tube and made it to the end of the gorge through the rapids of Liangjiarien and Mantianxing, meaning 'starstudded sky' and 'meteor shower'. Opinions differ as to whether a capsule qualifies as a raft at all, since it is the boating equivalent of going over Niagara Falls in a barrel.

The Yangtze had now been run from end to end, but not conquered. When Richard Bangs and John Yost of Sobek appeared on the scene a year later, in 1987, it was a comparative anticlimax. Sobek tackled a section of the river around Great Bend, where the rapids are considerable but not necessarily lethal.

The Great Bend of the Yangtze is a geological oddity. Situated one-third of the way down from the source, the river executes a remarkable hairpin bend, swirling from south to north between cliffs of limestone that at times are only 30m (100ft) apart. Two mountains soar high overhead – Jade Dragon Mountain (5596m; 18,360ft) to the south and Haba Snow Mountain (5396m; 17,705ft) to the north. Legend holds that a tiger pursued by hunters escaped by leaping from clifftop to clifftop in a single bound. Further downstream the river flattens out, though it continues to flow fast. Members of the Sobek expedition hiked the Tiger Leaping Gorge rather than attempting to run it with possibly fatal consequences. To their credit, the crew thus proved that safe rafting was achievable on the upper Yangtze, and a route on this section of the river is operated today by various rafting companies.

A SENSITIVE EXPLORATION OF CHINA'S RIVERS

As this is written, explorations are taking place on the headwaters of the Mekong and Salween rivers, cousins of the Tsangpo (Brahmaputra) rising in central China on the edge of the Plateau of Tibet, after which they flow southward and roughly parallel to each other. A leading protagonist on Chinese and Tibetan rivers is Colorado-based Peter Winn, a former Grand Canyon rafter. His nonprofit organization, Earth Science Expeditions, has gained the co-operation of the Chinese Academy of Sciences by field-checking geological maps for them. To ensure local support, Winn employs guides and interpreters who know the languages and their way around the land. The trips attract foreign participants who, like Winn himself, have fallen under the irresistible spell of the river dragons.

The term 'first descents in China' needs some qualifications. The Chinese have always used rivers for transportation, navigating mild whitewater stretches such as the Min River north of the city Chengdu (capital of China's Sichuan Province) and the Yangtze River downstream from Dukou city. Recently, many Chinese rivers have been surveyed by geologists in motorized Zodiacs for potential dam sites, but the major rapids were portaged.

Winn and his companions have now established in China that a 'first descent' means boating the rapids. On Winn's first trip down the upper Mekong in 1994, he reported that the Dragon's Teeth Rapid – formed by a major earthquake in 1988 – was the biggest he'd ever seen, bigger than any two rapids on the Grand Canyon combined. The party successfully ran it.

Winn has continued to visit China almost annually, maintaining links with the authorities and promoting rafting, but warning Westerners off areas that are sensitive for security reasons or are regarded as sacred, hidden kingdoms.

AN ECOLOGICAL BATTLE RAGES

The greatest hydro project the world has seen is under construction at the Three Gorges on the Yangtze River, which occur from Chongqing in central south China to the ancient city of Sandouping, a distance of 600km (375 miles). It has evoked dedicated opposition from within China itself, where detractors have been jailed. In the world at large, even funding organizations like the World Bank, which normally supports dam-building, have expressed doubts in line with the opposition from environmentalists. The founder of the modern Chinese industrial economy, Sun Yat-Sen, dreamed of such an enormous dam and the Chinese Communist government finally decided to build it. The goal is to propel change in an impoverished area of China, but the dam will displace between one and two million people. It will submerge irreplaceable cultural treasures and inundate some of the most beautiful scenery in China.

This project does not directly affect the whitewater sections of the Yangtze, which lie far upriver at the Tiger Leaping Gorge, Great Bend and other gorges. Yet river-runners have been at the forefront of efforts to spare the Yangtze from impoundment. They have seen other great rivers go under, from the Bio-Bio in Chile to the Selangor in Malaysia and Glen Canyon on the Colorado in the USA. Knowing as they do that a dam, once built, is as difficult to remove as the Pyramids, people who love wildly gushing rivers will instinctually reject the argument of 'benefits' of the damming. Counter-arguments are based on the long-term health of the land and heritage of communities.

In its campaigns against the dam, International Rivers Network (IRN) has been calling attention to the potentially disastrous environmental and social impacts of the project. In 1994, IRN and a coalition of US environmental, development and human rights groups lobbied the US administration to maintain a tough stand against the proposed dam. A year later the National Security Council concluded that the US government should stay clear of the Three Gorges Dam, and soon afterwards the US Export-Import Bank announced that they would not guarantee loans to US companies seeking contracts for its construction.

The Three Gorges Dam will not touch the upper Yangtze, but will indirectly affect it in many ways. If anything, the controversy will attract more visitors, and some may try rafting. Ecotourism, in other words, could benefit. Critics may resent this but tourism opens up opportunities for public education on the ecological and cultural value of rivers and the impact of dams.

ABOVE: *The Salween River, Tibet, which together with the Mekong flows parallel to the Tsangpo.*
LEFT: *Upper Gorge, Yangtze River.*

HIMALAYA

KALI GANDAKI * SUN KOSI AND DUDH KOSI * BRALDU * SUTLEJ * TSANGPO

Rivers that rise in Nepal are splendid, bursting between great rock abutments in a rush of noise and spray, then slowing to meander languidly through forests and plains. Names like the Karnali, Kali Gandaki, Trisuli, Marsiyandi, Sun Kosi and Tamur evoke a sense of mystery, like a whiff of incense with a tempting scent. Parallel to the Himalayan mountain range runs another, lower, range, closer to India, called the Mahabharat, with midland valleys in-between typified by the Kathmandu valley at a height of around 1300m (4300ft). Here, many of the great rivers flow parallel to the Himalaya for a while before cutting down to the lowlands, or Terai plain, bordering on India.

The snowmelt and monsoon rains create a wide selection of river trips, from rocky, fast rapids to easy rides set between jungle banks. Heavy rains expend themselves against the southern wall of the Himalaya and do not infiltrate the northern flank. The rivers tumble down from the Himalaya, passing temples, ashrams and terraced fields clinging to the mountainsides. In the lower reaches, enchanting forests of rhododendron, oaks and pines crowd the banks, while the snowy profiles of the great peaks tower overhead.

As abrupt as the change in the natural landscape is the cultural gap. In the verdant southern foothills, cheerful Hindu Gurung and Magar people grow crops and fish in the river, while in the north the more reserved Mongoloid tribes of Buddhist Manangis and Thakali manage a sparse living with their yak herds. Here, as elsewhere in the Himalaya and the Hindu Kush range, further to the northwest between Afghanistan and Pakistan, river valleys mark the routes to the interior. Overlanders and fly-in visitors will often combine hiking, rafting, mountain biking and even 'meditational holidays' – during which they enter a Buddhist retreat to contemplate the meaning of life.

In addition, of course, Nepal is the major staging area for mountain climbing expeditions into every corner of the central Himalaya. Much of the activity is concentrated around Kathmandu. Although it has been described as the spiritual adventure capital of the world, Kathmandu has become traffic-clogged as the number of visitors increases. The Annapurna hiking trail alone hosts 50,000 trekkers a year. Serious efforts are being made to clean up the Himalaya, but at least the rivers are not overcrowded.

ABOVE, LEFT TO RIGHT: *Kayaks are carried on the two-day trek in to the Karnali River, Nepal; the Kali Gandaki River runs near the foot of the world's second highest mountain, Annapurna; the Sun Kosi River is low and sluggish near its confluence with the Indrawati River, but don't be misled – it is a big, wild river.*
OPPOSITE: *A raft with seven people vanishes in El Wasto rapid on the Sun Kosi River, Nepal.*

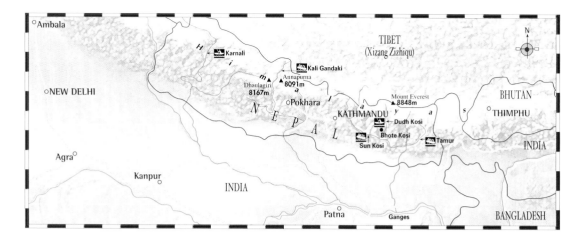

THE KALI GANDAKI, NEPAL

If the Himalaya today are fairly safe from the intrusions of powered boats (including jet-boats), it is because a popular ethos supports nonmotorized rafting and kayaking. But there are exceptions to the rule, depending on the spirit and the imagination of those who might dare to enter the mountain kingdom by water in small, powered boats.

In June 1972, a pair of explorers – French-born Michel Peissel and Briton Michael Alexander – stood on the banks of the Kali Gandaki River in the shadow of two of the highest peaks in the Himalaya, Annapurna

and Dhaulagiri. Cold, wet, and exultant, the men knew they had achieved one of the most audacious feats of exploration in modern times. They had crossed the Himalaya by river, from south to north, going upstream against the rapids in a 1930km (1200-mile) journey in two small single-seater hovercraft. The craft were as extraordinary in their own way as any spaceship. These boats floated inches over the water rather than on it, and could rock-hop without getting stuck.

Their three-month-long journey had taken them up nine different rivers, from India across Nepal to the borders of Tibet. Hugging the cliffs with the engine howl-

ing, passing waterfalls that gushed from straight under blue ice, and spattered by freezing spray, Peissel and Alexander penetrated what they called 'The Grandest Canyon'. They followed the route used by countless generations of traders, and now a favourite with backpackers. The Kali Gandaki, named after the terrifying Hindu goddess Kali, the devourer of time, is considered a holy river deserving of respect, and traverses what is known as the great Himalayan breach, bisecting the world's highest mountain range. The breach forms a staggering gorge which is nearly four times as deep as the Grand Canyon of the Colorado.

The river rises in an enclave of Nepal poking into Tibet, appearing at first as a flat and braided stream in a fairly wide valley. At Kalopani village the river drops off the roof of the world and cuts a profound chasm between Dhaulagiri (8167m; 26,796ft) to the west and Annapurna (8091m; 26,547ft) to the east. These Nepalese peaks rank in the world's top 10 highest mountains and are only 35km (22 miles) apart, yet the gorge separating them has a track running its entire length, used since ancient times as a commercial pathway and pilgrimage route. In less than a day's walk, the track passes through a tremendous range of ecological zones, from subtropical monsoon country to alpine, tundra-like desert. After its confluence with the Modi Khola, still in Nepal, the Kali Gandaki turns south through a wild area where tourists are almost unknown. The only road access along the 200km (125 miles) of river is at Ridi and Ramdi towns, where people are still unaccustomed to seeing boaters and will enthusiastically beckon visitors over for a chat. They live along terraces, hundreds high, above the water where the cooler air attracts fewer mosquitoes in the monsoon.

Michel Peissel, who sprang from French forebears and had grown up in Hertfordshire, England, had made his mark as an explorer of the Himalaya long before the hovercraft expedition on the Kali Gandaki. In 1964 he trekked into the remote kingdom of Mustang, also near

Annapurna, where he lived for several months and comprehensively recorded his contacts with local people; and in 1968 he was the first European to explore the eastern reaches of the restricted Buddhist mountain kingdom of Bhutan, east of Nepal. During the 1972 expedition upriver towards Tibet, whenever Peissel and Alexander came ashore they were immediately surrounded by a crowd of caravaners, peasants, herdsmen, and villagers with prayer wheels and Western-style umbrellas. Peissel surprised them all with his command of the Tibetan language, but the two must have seemed a weird spectacle, shivering in soaking baggy orange trousers and a pale blue anorak. To people who had never even seen a car, the hovercraft each travelled in

was an apparition only slightly less astonishing than a moon lander. With two motors, a steering stick and a seat for the driver, it was a strange combination of nautical, aero and car design. It consisted of an inflated hull, like a normal raft. Motor power drove a propeller which forced compressed air down through an intake vent to form an air cushion under the craft. On this cushion, the hovercraft, driven by another propeller that provided thrust from behind, glided over any moderately smooth surface. The hovercraft's arrival even attracted interest from the chief of Nepal's armed forces and the prime minister of the country, who evidently saw it as a possible means of rapid deployment and as general transport in a country with few roads.

Unfortunately, the hovercraft, for all its promise as an amphibious vehicle with the unique ability to cross water, ice and even loose sand with equal capability, has serious drawbacks, as Peissel discovered. At the best of times, it could not carry much weight. And on the Kali Gandaki, the hovercraft experienced increasing difficulty obtaining the lift needed to float it up over ground and water. The designers in the UK had not anticipated that the thin air and altitudes of nearly 3000m (9840ft) would cause constant drag on the craft.

While attempting an ascent of the Indrawati River, a whirling propeller cut off Peissel's fingertip; he nearly drowned when his craft overturned in rapids while Alexander followed, helpless, behind. The pair was

constantly worrying about the condition of the skirt that maintains the hovercraft's air cushion, as it could tear easily and fray away from the perpetual abrasion. With such drawbacks – as well as its noisiness – the hovercraft has never been adopted by river-runners as their craft of choice and is regarded, rather kindly, as a curiosity piloted by eccentrics.

The Kali Gandaki is (or was) probably the second most rafted river in Nepal, after the popular and accessible Trisuli. But in the late 1990s, the Kali Gandaki was dammed from just above the Modi Khola confluence to below Ridi Bazaar. The old five-day rafting trip was cut to three days, with the sad loss of a boisterous Class 4 rapid called Walk in the Dark. Not that everyone regretted the damming: a 'hang the environmentalists' campaign turned the ire of politicians on those who were thought to be opposing progress. Yet river-runners had to ask themselves, who exactly was walking in the dark?

SUN KOSI AND DUDH KOSI, NEPAL

Nepalese rivers that offer established routes and continue to attract whitewater enthusiasts are the Modi Kola, Marsyandi, Trisuli, Beri, Bhote Kosi, Arun, Tamur, Karnali, and Sun Kosi. Of the three major river systems in eastern Nepal – the Arun, the Sun Kosi and the Tamur – the best blend of excitement and action is provided by the Sun Kosi. Like its name, it is a sunny, happy river otherwise known as the River of Gold. The first descent of this river was carried out in 1981 by an Australian team led by John Wilde, after

the group spent some time in training on the Trisuli River. A full trip can take 7–10 days and it includes Grade 5 rapids. In September, with the monsoon lingering, the flow can reach 2800 cumecs (100,000cfs) and then the river truly deserves its reputation as one of the top 10 in the world. Between October and November it is mild, snaking through Nepal's middle hills more peacefully and allowing rafters more time to enjoy the scenic campsites. Some rivers on the steep gradients of the higher Himalaya have been described as 'damp cellar' staircases (continuous cascading rapids), better left to the true rapid addicts who thoroughly enjoy frigid glacial melt and are driven to test their boating skills against the most unnerving rivers.

One such river is the Dudh Kosi in central Nepal. The name means 'milk river', which is hardly surprising as it contains 130km (80 miles) of continuous and unpredictable white water during which distance it drops 3300m (10,800ft). The Dudh Kosi was made famous as The Relentless River of Everest in an award-winning video of that name. It recorded the 1976 British kayak expedition led by Dr Mike Jones, one of the UK's most intrepid paddlers. The expedition members started right at the source and stopped when it flattened out to normal Grade 3 rapids and became, in their view, boring. The film promoted paddling in the Himalaya as nothing had done before or has done since. In the video, Jones rescues his colleague, New Zealander Mick Hopkinson, in a stunning display of courage and kayaking expertise.

THESE PAGES: *The Upper Sun Kosi has tight channels packed with whitewater action: a raft drops into a hole, with passengers bunched forward to throw their maximum weight into the foam pile. The raft slews and recovers – but someone is overboard and is carried downstream before being rescued.*
RIGHT: *A laden local traveller negotiates a rickety bridge across the turbulent waters of the Dudh Kosi.*
FOLLOWING PAGES: *The Bhote Kosi River, flowing from Tibet, is a taxing, high-grade rafting trip.*

In those days, the state-of-the-art kayak was a long, rather racy-looking slalom boat with a fibreglass hull. Theirs were specially strengthened for Himalayan conditions, and were much heavier than normal. After a day of exhausting paddling down cascade-style rapids, the constant concentration took its toll on Hopkinson who relaxed for one brief moment and then took a spill in the maelstrom. Jones went after him, chasing him over several more drops where neither knew what was to come. Hopkinson was helped to safety, and though uninjured he was barely able to talk from shock and fatigue. The episode was captured by a camera Jones had taped to his helmet, and by another camera fortuitously positioned at a vantage point above the river. The edited footage made one of the most dramatic outdoor sequences ever filmed. Like the film *Deliverance* which had appeared on the movie circuit a few years earlier, it showed the ugly, obdurate side of rivers. It also had a tragic sequence a year later when Jones challenged the grim Braldu River and lost.

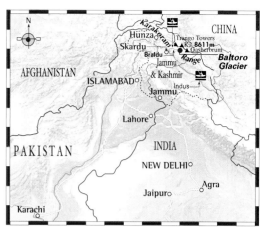

THE BRALDU, PAKISTAN

At the time Dr Mike Jones embarked on the 1976 Himalaya expedition, he was on his way to being acknowledged as the master of British kayaking. Although qualified as a doctor, his first love was the river. He had paddled the Grand Canyon, Alpine rivers, the Orinoco (Venezuela, South America) and Blue Nile, and was known everywhere for his madcap behaviour off the river and competent kayaking on it. Dave Manby, the youngest member of the 1976 Dudh Kosi expedition, had discovered on a previous Alpine trip what it was like to paddle with Jones. In one day it was not unusual to run three sections of serious white water, rush back to the campsite, cook a curry that included everything that was to hand, and then toddle off to the bar for some serious drinking.

Two years after the Dudh Kosi rescue, Jones decided to head back to Asia, this time to paddle rivers in the shadow of K2, at 8611m (28,253ft) the world's second highest mountain. The Karakoram range, which extends from Afghanistan through Pakistan to the Indian state of Jammu and Kashmir and then joins the Himalaya, contains some of the world's largest glaciers. It is from the Baltoro glacier at the foot of K2, in the heart of the Karakoram, that the Braldu River surges when spring and summer temperatures drive up the thaw.

The most outstanding scenic beauty in the region surrounds the Baltoro. From here, four 8000m (26,000ft) peaks can be seen in a wide circle, including Masherbrum,

OPPOSITE: *The Braldu River flows through the arid Karakoram; Gone village clings to its south bank.*
RIGHT: *Balti porters on a mountain trail high above the Braldu River, near Chango; the peaks of the Koser Gunge group of mountains rise in the east.*

Gasherbrum, K2 itself and the Trango Towers. The Braldu, however, born to glory, quickly descends to hell. It is one of the headwaters of the Indus, a frightening enough river itself, but the Braldu is worse. It rumbles through a grim cold valley where naked, tumbled grey boulders lie in turbid water cloudy with a freight of glacial grit. It looks like a killer, and so it proved to be. Perhaps because it was nobody's idea of a pleasant run downriver, Mike Jones managed to persuade his old team to join him once more for a really hard-bitten trip that would strip away their complacency. Arrogance possibly took hold; more likely it was just bad luck, but on a trial run down the Braldu to warm up for things to come, Jones once again attempted to rescue a fellow paddler in trouble, and he himself drowned. The sobered group left the river.

Amazingly, in 1983 Dave Manby returned to the Karakoram determined to re-run the Braldu — alone. Asked why he did it, he replied glibly that he had some 'unfinished business' with the brute that killed his friend. He had the opportunity to study the cliff-face fronting on the current where Mike Jones had disappeared. A long undercut sliced into the cliff, and here almost certainly, at the higher level they had run it in 1978, Jones must have been sucked in with no hope of escape. Manby now took up the crusade. On a casual paddle on the first afternoon of his run he was nearly killed too. Paddling over an innocuous-looking drop, Manby found himself pinned in the kayak with the full force of the river on his back. He nearly broke both knees falling forward out of the cockpit. He managed to get to the side of the river and later retrieved his kayak which had luckily washed up on the bank, but he could not stand up straight afterwards; he beat a hellish retreat from the Braldu with legs that hardly worked and buckled under him as he attempted to hike out.

Manby went on to establish a rafting operation on the Coruh River in Turkey (see p87). Mick Hopkinson, whose life Jones had saved on the Dudh Kosi, set up swiftwater rescue classes in New Zealand. Both remained at the cutting edge of international paddling. Manby quotes the words of Doug Ammons, a close kayaking friend: 'We aren't crazy. We aren't seeking thrills. We just want the truth. Confronting such challenges gives you the best answers you can look for in life.'

RIVERS OF INDIA AND PAKISTAN

Nepal is not alone in offering a vast assortment of rivers. It is flanked by several administrative divisions of India. To the northwest are Kashmir, Himachal Pradesh and Uttar Pradesh where the mighty Indus and Ganges rivers cut through the Himalaya from their origins in Tibet. The west tends to be very dry; the further east you go, the wetter it becomes, filling rivers like the Brahmaputra, Teesta and Pho Chu with huge volumes of water destined for the vulnerable flood plains of Assam and Bangladesh.

The rivers are almost too numerous to mention. Upper sections of the Indus and the Ganges are rafted and kayaked, but most of the action is focused more to the east in Nepal and Sikkim. The skyline in Sikkim is dominated by the solemn massif of Kangchenjunga peak, the third highest mountain in the world at 8598m (28,209ft), with no less than five peaks. In deference to local religious beliefs, mountaineers usually stop a few metres short of the main summit.

For river-runners there are no such complications. The Tamur River drains the snows of Kangchenjunga, and on the lower slopes rafting groups can expect to encounter 130 rapids over 120km (75 miles), one of the most thrilling commercially rafted descents in Nepal. There is no taboo, either, against kayaking on the many torrents spilling down the slopes of Sikkim into the Chumbi Valley. Here the Teesta River has drawn increasing numbers of rafters since the kingdom was opened to international visitors in 1978.

THE SUTLEJ

It is thought that only three archaic rivers existed before the Himalaya arose from the collison of continents: those that geologists call the Sindhu (Indus), Shatadru (Sutlej) and Brahmaputra (Tsangpo). All sprang from Lake La'nga in southwestern Tibet, and still do rise in its immediate environs. The Sindhu flows away to the northwest and then turns suddenly southward through a gap in the Hindu Kush. The Brahmaputra subsides eastwards, channelled between the Tibetan Plateau and the Himalaya. The Shatadru, meanwhile, strikes west-southwest through Himalayan gorges, crosses Himachal Pradesh state and enters the arid plains of the Punjab. It is the longest of the so-called 'five rivers' that converge finally to make up the main Indus River, cradle of the culture of ancient Indus, one of the primal civilizations of the world along with Mesopotamia and Egypt. The ancient silk route followed the Sutlej River, which forms the natural boundary between India and Tibet (now China). The ancient trade route runs most of its length from the plains of India to Tibet. The Sutlej had remained strangely unknown to modern boaters – strangely because the Tsangpo, Karnali, Indus and Sutlej all derive from the same region around Mount Kailas, and the other three have been the focus of kayakers for years.

In 1999, British paddler Allan Ellard, veteran of many Himalayan first descents, decided to set the record straight. He and several friends tackled the gorges, choked with summer snowmelt, from near the border between Tibet and India, down to the town of Rampur, a distance of 170km (106 miles).

Himachal Pradesh lived up to its name of 'snowy mountain state', with spring runoff from the surrounding peaks pushing the flow rate to roughly 2000 cumecs (7000cfs) – 'Ridiculous', to quote Ellard, who set off nervously down the unexplored corridor hemmed in by peaks and canyon walls. The granite bedrock base was littered with polished boulders, shed by the surrounding heights. Occasionally the canyon would narrow and pinch the Sutlej to a handful of metres wide, at an unimaginable depth of water. The rapids got bigger, the thrills wilder, but at the end Ellard concluded that the river was amazing because it was consistently runnable, except for a few stretches which could be portaged with much effort.

PREVIOUS PAGES: *On a 1989 expedition on the Moksu River in Pakistan, an oar boat is slammed hard against a rockface while crew members scramble to avoid being crushed.*
OPPOSITE: *The Rhondu Gorges of the Indus River in Pakistan carved by massive snowmelt.*
ABOVE: *Jaw-jutting determination on the Sutlej.*

RIVERS OF TIBET

Regarded as the roof of the world, Tibet has an average elevation of more than 4800m (15,750ft) and despite the fact that it lies in a rain shadow, it is the main watershed of Asia. The landscape is arid, parched by the sun and searingly cold winds, and the distances are always greater than they seem because the air is so dry and uncompromisingly clear. A sparse population survives on yak and goat milk, tilling ridiculously unyielding patches of grey earth. Extremes of climate, particularly the cold winters, make conditions inhospitable and the life is harsh indeed. The people are cheerful, devout Buddhists, and their love of life ensures they are both curious about, and hospitable towards, foreigners.

Tibet is the source of the Indus, Tsangpo/Brahmaputra, Salween, Mekong, and Yangtze, and not surprisingly, all this water has produced a long history of conflict and conquest, empire-building and resistance. When Buddha, the sixth-century Indian philosopher, was living in India, and Chinese philosphers Confucius and Lao-tzu in China, Tibetan raiders invaded central China and continued to menace the celestial empire for many centuries. Only the Mongol Khans succeeded in driving them back.

Curiously, it has been surmised that the technology of inflatable rafting may well have been born in this part of Asia. To ferry across the rivers, and for purposes of trade, the people of the region have boated for many centuries. According to Mongol oral tradition, 'inflatable rafts' — consisting of blown-up animal skins — were used in invasions and counter-invasions to ferry men and supplies across the rivers. A single man could lie on these inflatables and paddle to the other side, rather like a floating mattress, or lilo. In some cases a platform was laid across several of the skins to make a true raft that was poled along, dragged by mules or navigated by means of sweep oars. Blow-up animals are still used in northern India today — it is a comical sight to spot a man walking with a four-legged air balloon animal strapped to his back, rather like a large aquatic toy.

The rivers on the Tibetan roof of the world are like the landscape: bleak, isolated and mystical. The nomads who dwell on the dusty, exposed plains, living in makeshift tents, are prey to many strange and wonderful imaginings. In the closing years of the 20th century, a strikingly handsome 14-year-old nomad boy was identified by monks as the Karmapa Lama, reborn leader

of one of Tibetan Buddhism's four main sects. It was said that at his birth, three suns had appeared beneath a magical rainbow; at seven years old, he would disappear into the mountains to ride on the backs of goats and jackals. Mythology interweaves with reality in this mountain wilderness where snowfed rivers are born amid awesome rock spires.

THE TSANGPO (BRAHMAPUTRA)

The Brahmaputra River (Sanskrit for 'son of Brahma'), is one of the holy rivers rising near the citadel-shaped Mount Kailas, said to be the birthplace of the Hindu god Shiva, whose hair formed the four great rivers: Brahmaputra, Indus, Karnali and Sutlej. The river's upper, Tibetan, section is known as the Tsangpo but the name changes to the Brahmaputra as it enters the Arunachal Pradesh and Assam states of India.

The Tsangpo runs west to east before turning south into easternmost India. It then crosses into Bangladesh, and finally flushes into the Bay of Bengal. For much of its distance it is fairly flat, incised into a long, linear valley that is clearly visible in Space Shuttle photo-

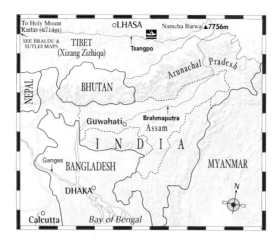

graphs, marking the geological collision line of the Eurasian and Indian tectonic plates.

James Hilton's 1933 novel, *Lost Horizon*, wove a fantasy around the traditional Tibetan legend of a sacred sanctuary, called a *beyul*, that lay hidden within a secluded Himalayan valley and was unknown to ordinary mortals. It was the land of Shangri-La, concealed behind a portal of rock whose threshold no strangers had ever crossed. Here was a paradise of gardens where time no longer existed and people lived tranquilly for hundreds of years. The course of the

Tsangpo/Brahmaputra seems to substantiate the legend of Shangri-La – intimating it is not without foundation in geographic reality.

In November 1998, American explorer Ian Baker and his 10-man expedition reached a previously uncharted waterfall on the Tsangpo, a good way down its course and shortly before it turns towards India. They espied a rock portal leading into a mysterious valley, and here at last, after a search of five years, Baker felt that he had found the route into the *beyul* of Pemako, 'the valley of the blue moon' – the land of Shangri-La. Directions deciphered from eighth-century Buddhist texts had pointed the way; Baker had painstakingly decoded them and found a description of three waterfalls, the middle one being so awe-inspiring it seemed worth finding as it might be the doorway to Pamako.

In this wilderness region of eastern Tibet, the famed Tsangpo gorges contain hundreds of rapids and falls over a distance of about 50km (30 miles), but for centuries the Monpa hunters who inhabit the lower Tsangpo valley had guarded the area from outsiders. It was finally they who led Baker to the innermost gorge.

Baker's discovery of the waterfall — which he named the Hidden Falls — has whetted the appetites of river-runners. This section of the river is not to be toyed with, for aerial photographs show the Tsangpo to be a night-marish trench choked with Grade 6 rapids churning its jade waters to snow-white foam. The river makes a tight hairpin bend around the impressive peak of Namcha Barwa and heads for a break in the great Himalayan escarpment. At his moment of success, Baker was to be disappointed. Though he was able to confirm the riddle of the waterfall, he and the others were unable to enter the portal. Since then China has closed Pamako to further foreign exploration, citing security considerations in eastern Tibet. Thus the mystery remains intact. Perhaps it is rightly so, for as Baker himself has said, in every culture there is a dream of some sanctuary where the best of civilization can be preserved, untouched.

For pioneering river-runners, it was never easy to get into Tibet, and some chose to become 'trespaddlers' without official permission. American kayakers Arlene Burns and Dan Dixon (nicknamed Greystoke after Tarzan, Lord of the Apes) decided to avoid the US$500,000 permit fee demanded by the Chinese government for a first descent, and set out to paddle the Tsangpo from its source near Mount Kailas. That they never quite found the source was no fault of theirs: they spent a month crisscrossing the Tibetan tundra suffering huge privations of cold and hunger. A party of Chinese surveyors gave them a lift into the vast emptiness of the Tibetan plateau and then abandoned them where no further help was available. They paddled across the sacred Lake Manasarovar at an altitude of some 4500m (14,800ft), within sight of Mount Kailas, and here nearly perished in a blizzard. Finally the pair did manage to reach the Tsangpo below the point where they had originally crossed it on their way to seek the source, and at last headed off downriver. But then a chance encounter with trekkers brought Arlene news that her boyfriend would be awaiting her in Bangkok. She left, and Greystoke carried on alone through treacherous gorges, paddling the rapids by night and sleeping in caves during the day, haunted by fear of the Chinese authorities. When his kayak was stolen near Lhasa he abandoned the trip.

Outlaws were the reason for a rafting trip of a very different, official, complexion that was successfully completed down the Tsangpo/Brahamaputra in 1992. The Indo-Tibetan Border Police, an Indian unit tasked with checking illegal immigration and smuggling, joined forces with the Himalayan Association of Japan to send a rafting party down some 1400km (870 miles). Under their Indian leader, 'SP' Chamoli, an experienced Himalayan explorer, they proceeded from Geling on the border of China (Tibet) to Dhubri on the middle course of the Brahmaputra in Assam province. There was plenty of whitewater action in the upper reaches though the river began to run out of steam after that. Still, the expedition helped the authorities plan for flood disaster management in the future.

PREVIOUS PAGES: *Villagers generally welcome water-borne adventurers to the Himalayan rivers.*
LEFT: *The Tsangpo River near Gyatsa on the high, arid Tibetan Plateau; the Tsangpo gorges have been dubbed the 'Mount Everest of Gorges'.*
BELOW: *Sun Kosi River, Nepal.*

THE POWERFUL MYTHOLOGY OF RIVERS

River legends and tales of adventure have always fascinated us, perhaps because they sum up the notion that rivers put us in touch with the primal energy and chaos of the universe. In 'The Dry Salvages' the poet T S Eliot mused, 'The river is within us, a strong brown god – sullen, untamed and intractable'.

When the long hot summer of the Indian mainland draws to a close, Indra, the king of the gods, appears to drive off the drought demons. In Vedic and later Hindu mythology, Indra ('he who flings thunderbolts') brings the cloud cattle to graze on the slopes of the Himalaya. In so doing he causes the 'five rivers' to swell with his longed-for monsoon.

Although we can never know for sure what rivers the ancient tale-tellers were describing, they were probably referring to the headwaters of the Indus – the Chenab, Ravi and Sutlej (in modern-day Pakistan) – as well as the Ganges in India and possibly the Brahmaputra in Bangladesh. Indra's holy name is preserved in the names of the Indus River and India itself. Like many rivergods, past and present, Indra was both worshipped and feared. His life-giving spirit brought the rice harvest, but his devastating floods carried victims into the great darkness beyond the river.

Further afield, on the African continent, other rivers collect local lore as rainforests gather moss. On the Zambezi River in Southern Africa, the river sprite Nyaminyami is a divinity of the Tsonga people, who believe that he controls life on the river. With the body of a snake and the head of a fish, it is said that when Nyaminyami appears, it is like a whirlwind over the water. Like the Loch Ness Monster and the dragon of the Yangtze river, he is seen only by the lucky few.

To the Greeks, the River Styx was the sacred river that flowed seven times around Hades (a haven in the underworld harbouring the souls of the dead), and had to be crossed by all souls on their way to the underworld. Chilling and dark, the Styx was also a source of fertility and guarantor of solemn oaths. The gods would take a cup of water from the river and swear by it while pouring it onto the earth to ensure the success of their schemes.

THE EAST, AUSTRALIA & NEW ZEALAND

ALAS * PADAS * STRICKLAND * NORTH JOHNSTONE * FRANKLIN * WAIKATO * CLARENCE

The entire region stretching from Indonesia to Oceania (the lands of the South and Central Pacific) is rich in rivers. Informally known as Austronesia, this swatch of planet Earth, framed by the Indian and Pacific oceans, encompasses nearly every kind of ecological zone from monsoon cloud forest through desert to temperate grassland and subpolar ice fields. The variety of river sights and cultural experiences seems equally limitless.

Gibbons and orang-utans hang in the jungle beside the wild Asahan River in Sumatra (Indonesia), a few degrees north of the equator. On Viti Levu island in Fiji, the Wainikoroiluva (Luva) River slices a deep chasm through the Namosi Highlands where waterfalls plummet out of the rainforest. On the broad Murray River in New South Wales (Australia), Mississippi-style paddle steamers ply the waters, packed with tourists; and in the chilly confines of the Southern Alps in New Zealand, kayakers tackle the frenetic Arahura River where the rapids have forbidding names like Cesspit and Curtain Call.

The immense spread of Indonesia and its neighbour, Malaysia, falling within a zone of torrential and perpetual rainfall, offers exceptional opportunities for whitewater boating. International paddlers have barely dipped their blades in the rivers of Borneo, Sulawesi and Irian Jaya; and while the rivers of Sumatra and Papua New Guinea are better known, some have fearsome reputations that keep all but the brave away.

The countries that make up the complex of Australasia are mainly Australia, the Cook Islands, Micronesia, New Zealand, Papua New Guinea and Tonga. The geology comprises some of the oldest rocks in the world in Australia's Outback, with some of the newest volcanic and faulted mountains occurring in the Alpine Fault Zone of New Zealand.

Not surprisingly, some of the world's greatest whitewater experts have sprung from Australia and New Zealand — countries very different in character but passionate about the importance of adventure in peoples' lives. The characteristic twang of their accents is heard everywhere above the roar of rapids. Generations of paddlers from 'Down Under' and 'Kiwiland' have left their native shores to pioneer routes in the Himalayas, Central Asia, Africa and South America, and are widely admired.

ABOVE, LEFT TO RIGHT: *Kayakers experience a snowstorm during a trip on the Karamea River, New Zealand; Skippers Canyon in the Shotover River valley, near Queenstown; the Kaituna River in the North Island, New Zealand.*
OPPOSITE: *A short but exciting kayak run is to be had down the Hooker River in the South Island's Aoraki/Mount Cook National Park. The river pours from near the foot of Aoraki/Mount Cook into Lake Pukaki (a Maori term meaning 'bunched-up water').*

RAFTING IN THAILAND

Rapids vary in size and strength – some are huge and terrifying, others are so small they hardly break the surface of the water, though the current may be swift. In Thailand, which is not very mountainous, very few rivers run white, but rafting on bamboo platforms amid charming jungle scenery is a popular adventure attraction. Rafters do not sit but stand with wet feet, poling the somewhat unseaworthy craft along. The numerous rivers hiss and bubble between walls of green, with the chance of spotting pythons, buffaloes, and even the rare leopard in the wildlife sanctuaries.

The standard Thai raft consists of many thick bamboo poles lashed together with a structure in the middle of the frame for tying luggage to. If the raft bumps on rocks and tipples over, everything gets wet so valuables and photo equipment are carried in waterproof bags as in conventional whitewater rafting.

One of the most popular trips is along the Sangkhalia River, an hour's drive from the provincial centre of Kanchanaburi, in the foothills of the Bilauktaung Range on the border with Myanmar (Burma). The raft journey concludes with an elephant ride and a jungle hike and finally ends at the historic Three Pagodas Pass on the border. Kanchanaburi Province is the site of the world-famous Bridge Over the River Kwai immortalized in books and movies, and of the Death Railway built by Allied prisoners of the Japanese in World War II. This river is bamboo rafted too.

A trip on the Pai River in the northwest of the country, from Ban Nam Khong to Mae Hong Song town, takes about five hours, passing a hot spring well, waterfalls and an enchanting cave. There are 15 small rapids with lengths that vary between 50 and 300m (165 and 1000ft). Among the few genuine whitewater rivers in Thailand is the rocky, fast-flowing Mae Taeng River in mountainous Chiang Mai Province. This river is filled with lots of sharp bends and rapids. Here too, however, small ruggedly constructed bamboo rafts are used for those who don't mind a dunking.

INDONESIA

THE ALAS, SUMATRA

The Indonesians refer to their string of 17,000-plus islands as Tanah Air Kita, 'our earth and water'. Dominated by a spine of volcanic mountains, the archipelago straggles over 5000km (3000 miles), from tropical Asia into the Pacific, harbouring some of the most unforgettable river experiences in the world. The untamed interior of Sumatra is one of the last natural preserves of Asian tigers, Indonesian rhinoceroses, and the orang-utan. A video entitled 'The River of the Red Ape' (1985) was shot during the first descent of the unexplored Alas River, led by the American-based Sobek rafting outfit. It featured primatologist Michael Ghiglieri, a protégé of Jane Goodall who has since become known for his view that Man can learn from the apes because human nature has a dark side — a propensity towards random violence — that is largely missing from other primate behaviours.

Once the Alas had been pioneered it became a popular rafting venue. Meeting at Medan, the principal city of northwestern Sumatra which is surrounded by tea and tobacco plantations, paddlers are transported to the river canyon which runs through the Gunung Leuser National Park. A stretch of rapids up to Class 3+ occurs in the upper section, followed by placid floating down the lower end where the silence is broken only by forest sounds. In the early mornings, the eerie and unforgettable 'song of Siamang', the call of the black gibbon, echoes through the river's amphitheatre. The wild Alas has run its course.

Ultimately, at the confluence of the Renun and Alas rivers, upmarket river tour operators offer candlelit dinners, wine and colourful spicy Eastern dishes.

Opposite: *Typical log raft on Thailand's Pai River.*
Left: *Paddlers on the Alas River rescue their raft.*

NEW GUINEA

The far eastern border of Indonesia is in New Guinea, the world's second largest island after Greenland, partitioned between the Indonesian province of Irian Jaya ('triumph of the Irian') and the independent state of Papua New Guinea. The island has long fascinated explorers and anthropologists. It is fringed by welcoming tropical beaches, with vast swamps occupying the sweltering plains behind. Further in, the island's central spine – known as the Central Range – is darkly forbidding, crowded with green peaks that disappear into perpetual cloud cover. In this country of wild beauty, the major rivers carry enormous volumes of water from the continual monsoon rains. The highlands rise to 5000m (16,400ft) and are dissected by thousands of river valleys, each barred from the next by precipitous and impassable spurs. They effectively cut off whole populations of living creatures from one another.

Although only four million people live in Papua New Guinea, at least 700 different languages are spoken. No two regions are alike and the astounding complexity has earned New Guinea the name, Land of a Thousand Cultures. The indigenous people belong to three principal groups: the Negritos, Melanesians, and Papuans, while some in the highlands are pygmies with a unique ethnic lineage. About half a million hunter-gatherers live in the hills and swamps, breeding domesticated pigs and spearing wild ones, growing coconuts, yams and bananas, and fishing.

During the past two centuries, New Guinea has been a magnet for map-makers, social scientists and curiosity-seekers with a taste for the truly exotic. Modern recreational paddlers who are drawn by the unknown have come to this strange environment. Miners and developers have come too, lured by profit and the prospect of social upliftment for peoples who were, until very recently, cannibals and head-hunters.

The islanders were not much bothered by visitors until aircraft began to overfly central New Guinea to get a fix on possible routes into the interior. Though government survey maps still showed large blank areas due to invisibility beneath the clouds, small but significant numbers of land travellers managed to push roadways through the green barriers of vegetation. Modern river-runners have focused their attention on the monstrous scale of the rivers themselves.

THE THREAT OF PROGRESS

As late as the 1960s, the Asmat tribe living in New Guinea's rainforests still indulged in cannibalism, according to visiting anthropologists. Recent documentation has played down this sensational claim, emphasizing instead that the tribes have well-developed spiritual systems, expressed, for instance, in refined wood carvings. The denials have done little to dent the fearsome reputation of the New Guineans. Even their carvings are said to have malign power, capable of paralyzing enemies.

But the New Guineans look increasingly like victims themselves. Their habitat is endangered by logging, mining and clear-cutting for agriculture. According to Greenpeace, vast new areas of rainforest are destined for destruction as the official PNG Forest Authority doles out concessions. The rivers, too, are threatened.

A coalition of environmental groups and community-based organizations has alleged for years that the Porgera gold mine in the Enga Province of Papua New Guinea poses a risk to the health of local people and riverine life. Owned by Placer Dome, the mine at Porgera is one of the largest and most profitable gold mines in the world. Reports said it was discharging high levels of waste disposal into the Maiapam–Strickland river system, feeding into the Fly River in the Papuan lowlands. Along with the rock waste, the tailings included metal sulphides and hydroxides such as ferro-cyanide which would poison subsistence gardens and fisheries along the rivers. The PNG government has a share in the mine, along with Australian-based Orogen Minerals Ltd. Porgera responded to protests by denying any responsibility for downstream deaths or illness, which it claimed were due to causes other than poisoning by the mine tailings. The owners argued that the discharges were necessary because it was not feasible to build a tailings dam due to unstable geology, rainfall of 3500mm (138in) per year, and steep terrain.

Still, the mine operators reportedly said they would begin phasing out the tailings from 1996. Three years later a report by the NGO coalition stated there had been 'increasing, not decreasing, negative impact on the river system and its human inhabitants'. The company disputed the allegations and assured the public it was monitoring water quality and complying with all statutory standards. Meantime, it signed an agreement to develop a housing estate near the mine so that employees could settle down rather than commute from afar.

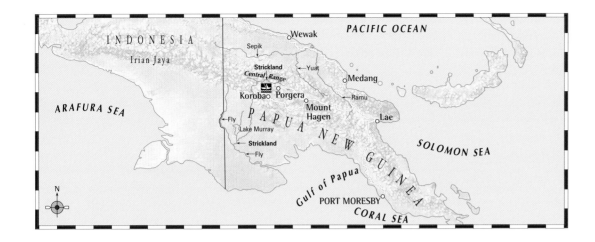

run is down the Padas River, near the capital of Sabah State in the Malaysian sector. Located south of the provincial capital of Kota Kinabalu, the Padas is one of the rivers flowing from the deeply contoured Crocker Range and it contains boulder-strewn waterways set amidst lush, tranquil forests. Eight to eleven hours of nerve-tingling excitement await those keen to try it, and to add to the attraction the only way in is by diesel train along the spectacular Padas gorge surrounded by a chorus of sounds from exotic birds and insects.

One may be lucky enough to catch sight of an orang-utan, protected in several sanctuaries in Borneo. Life is generally very unhurried for these large primates, but they are being harried to extinction. Although in prehistoric times there were orang-utans on the Asian mainland, today they are found in just a few restricted areas of Borneo and Sumatra.

Borneo is a veritable paradise of exotic species. Living in the rainforests are the proboscis monkey, longtail macaque, wild boar, sambhar deer and monitor lizards.

THE PADAS, BORNEO

The rivers of Malaysia, Indonesia and the Philippines — all areas of volcanic geology, high rainfall and thick fertile vegetation — have a daunting reputation for adrenaline-pumping, muscle-straining action, with the presence of crocodiles in many places to spice up the fear of falling in. The rivers are often choked with jungle detritus and other nasty tangled vegetation like deadly barbed vine creepers. Colourful birds flit through the shadows, and in places like the island of Borneo, the long-armed, red-haired orang-utans move slowly through the treetops uttering loud mating calls.

Borneo, the third largest island in the world, has not been fully explored for its whitewater offerings. Mountainous, with few roads, and drenched by the northeast monsoon, its landscape and humid climate have tended to keep all but the most determined river explorers out of the deep interior. Today, however, rafters and kayakers are boldly going where none have gone before, and the World Wide Web is buzzing with tales of first descents in Borneo and its neighbouring tropical islands.

Borneo is divided between Malaysia, Indonesia and the tiny state of Brunei. A popular commercial rafting

BELOW: *The Padas River offers rafting routes through the mist-wreathed fertile forests of Sabah, Borneo.*

THE STRICKLAND, PAPUA NEW GUINEA

There could hardly be a more mysterious and frightening river than the Strickland, which cuts a gorge through the Auagum mountain range in central Papua New Guinea (PNG). Only when the Strickland River became the focus of an international campaign against alleged cyanide pollution from gold mining at Porgera (see p126) did boaters realize that the wildest of rivers was also, possibly, one of the sickest, afflicted with a disease of industrial civilization.

The grim canyon slashed in the landscape by the immense run-off of the Strickland — combined with its steep gradient — is visible from the air, but most of it has never yet been successfully boated. Rising in the very heart of the island, the Strickland swiftly declines by more than 1000m (3300ft) in a matter of 30km (20 miles) before joining the Fly River which drains into the Coral Sea.

At the end of the 1970s, the Strickland was tackled in typically military fashion by one of the UK's most intrepid explorers, Royal Engineer Colonel John Blashford-Snell, as part of Operation Drake, a two-year youth development programme. Blashford-Snell had been the successful leader of the first descent of the Congo River (then Zaïre) in Central Africa and of a Blue Nile expedition in 1968. Nicknamed Blashers by colleagues, he was not able to conquer the Strickland. His heavily-financed expedition lost one of its two rafts and he was forced to give up after 45km (28 miles). Eight men waited three days on a ledge before helicopters arrived to evacuate the team.

In the 1990s another group of boaters appeared on the river, this time four German kayakers, determined to complete a first descent of its course. They flew into Mount Hagen town, lying about 500km (300 miles) direct from the capital, Port Moresby. The town is hemmed in by jungle thickets on the highlands between Mount Hagen and Onim Peak, and it was only by helicopter that they were able to get a look at the Strickland canyon stretching through the jungle, its rocks wet and shiny from ground water.

RIGHT: *The wild forbidding beauty of Papua New Guinea makes it an exotic destination for rafters, who are destined to get their share of excitement on rivers constantly fed by heavy monsoon rains.*

Helicopters overflew the river every few days from the Porgera mine. With the co-operation of the mine they chartered one and planned a series of exact checkpoints at which the pilots could meet them. This was wise planning. Once they were dropped, storms in the mountains caused the river to rise continually. On reaching the Strickland ravine, nervousness took hold of the kayakers. The volume of the river quadrupled overnight, and the foaming, dark brown rapids were so fast that there was little chance to manoeuvre or to miss the uprooted tree trunks floating in the flood. Their veins froze as they hit a gigantic rapid, a combination of huge breakers and deep holes. Lukas, one of the four Germans, came out of his kayak and was tumbled downstream after being held in a recycling hole. He vanished, and the remaining three spent a terrified night, unable to sleep while watching the river rise another metre.

Next morning came the 'pok-pok-pok' compression roar of a helicopter, the door opened and Lukas, whom they had given up for dead, stepped out. He had been washed for miles downriver, choking on muddy water, and had barely clawed his way up the bank to spend the night in a cave, drinking water from puddles. An alert helicopter pilot saw a naked Lukas waving from a rock and imagined he was the only survivor of the four that had been flown to the river with their kayaks. The party was joyfully reunited, but once again the Strickland had overwhelmed its challengers; the trip was abandoned.

Daring is the chief constituent of extreme river adventures like the Strickland exploration, but it is not everything. Boaters at the ends of the earth today rely on a combination of audacity, a high level of river-running skills, rugged equipment, and good information and backup. Vastly improved maps based on satellite imagery have made it possible to study areas that were previously little more than blanks. Helicopters or 4x4s convey the adventurers directly to the scene of action. It all makes adventure seem so much easier, especially if rescue and emergency recovery are feasible. Yet, at the cutting edge of whitewater adventure there is still the risk of serious injury and death. The Strickland paddlers came out alive not just through luck but because they were tough-minded and experienced enough to handle the worst scenarios and survive.

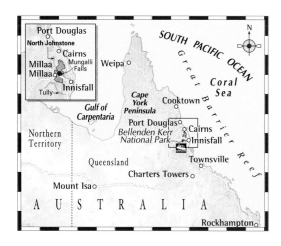

AUSTRALIA & NEW ZEALAND

Despite Australia's largely arid, isolated interior, plenty of rain falls along the country's coasts, particularly in the northeastern forest zone around Cairns and the Cape York Peninsula. Raftable rivers come charging down the flanks of the Great Dividing Range to the coastline made famous by the Great Barrier Reef.

Many more rivers lie to the south, feeding the mighty Murray River, Australia's longest, which begins near Mount Koskiuszko and then flows 2590km (1600 miles) through rolling countryside into Lake Alexandria, near Adelaide. The Murray has a special place in the Aboriginal legends of the Dreamtime, and today its tributaries and lakes provide a nesting place for rare birdlife, as well as some of the best vineyards in Australia. Tasmania's Franklin River is perhaps the jewel in the crown, much prized by Australians as it was saved from damming by a national campaign that shook the government to its foundations.

The rivers tell the story of Australia's deep and turbulent history. Cooktown, to the north of Cairns, lies on the Endeavour River where in 1770 Captain James Cook beached his battered ship for barnacle removal after a voyage halfway around the world. Aboriginal tribes set fire to Cook's camp when the English failed to acknowledge historic tribal territorial rights to marine resources. The steady increase of white settlement generated more than a century of Aboriginal resistance, much of it focused around rivers and billabongs. Australia's indigenous human inhabitants were superstitious about rivers, rightly so. The rivers support one of the oddest of all aquatic creatures, the platypus. Platypuses hatch from an egg like reptiles and have an electronic 'radar' system somewhat like bats to find food in the water with their eyes closed.

THE NORTH JOHNSTONE, AUSTRALIA

In earlier days, white settlers who encamped along the Johnstone River, near today's town of Cairns, stripped the area of its natural food resources for agriculture and forestry. This initiated Aborigine attacks during which the camps were pillaged and boats burned or removed.

Modern-day boaters on the Johnstone, which offers awesome boating on its northern reaches, will wonder at the strange world-view of the indigenous peoples whose ancient culture remains enigmatic to Westerners. Cairns is today a fast-growing town and regarded as the southern gateway to the wild, sparsely inhabited Cape York Peninsula. Helicopters drop parties in the gorge and the only way out is by water. The river carves its way between volcanic walls, giving rafters a rare glimpse of an untouched part of North Queensland's World Heritage area. It is here that Queensland found its state floral emblem, the Cooktown Orchid. The hybrid occurs from the Johnstone River to the Iron Range, which cuts off the rainforests from the drier interior.

Cairns is also the gateway to the Great Barrier Reef Marine Park, and therefore a centre for big-game fishing, but it is also the hometown of river-running, Aussie-style. Much heavy rain falls along the Atherton Plateau and the Great Dividing Range, southeast of Cairns, creating voluminous rivers. The Barron River, a perfect introduction to the sport, has exciting Grade 3 rapids. The wilder Tully River offers Grade 4 and 5, with more than 40 rapids in an almost continuous sequence as the river pummels a circuit around Mount Tyson.

THE NEPEAN – AN OLYMPIC COURSE FOR AUSTRALIA

Further south, near Sydney, a world class artificial whitewater course was built on the Nepean River for the 2000 Olympic Games. The Nepean rises in the uplands west of Wollongong (south of Sydney) and flows northward past Camden to its junction with the Warragamba River near Wallacia.

The names alone emphasize the strangeness of whitewater in these climes. Before European settlement the Nepean River was a major source of food for Aborigines, who caught fish in its waters and dug for wild yams along its banks. In the early years of the British colony of Australia, the valley was known as 'the granary' because of its rich soils, and indeed there were times that its produce kept the fledgling colony alive. Nowadays it provides the open water for recreational boating.

The artificial course resembles a rapid-filled stream, using water pumped from the regatta lake on the Nepean. With a maximum flow rate of 12 cumecs (5200cfs), the course is surrounded by natural grassed banks allowing for grandstand seating of up to 10,000 spectators.

THE FRANKLIN, TASMANIA (AUSTRALIA)

Tasmania, Australia's island state lying off the continent's southeastern reaches, is famous mainly for its Tasmanian Devil – a black-coated, meat-eating marsupial larger than a bulldog, with powerful jaws and a foul temper. These Tasmanian Devils once roamed all over Australia but are now confined to the island state. Tasmania has afforded protection to a marvellous river system that was threatened by the proposed construction of a hydroelectric power station in 1979.

The Franklin River starts in subalpine lands on the flanks of the Cradle Mountain–St Clair National Park. It descends through Frenchmans Cap National Park, fringed by rainforests, then skirts the base of quartz peaks and the Kutikina limestone caves. The caves were inhabited by Aborigines during the last ice age and they constitute an important archaeological site. Thousand-year Huon Pines tower over the rushing narrows.

Swelled by large tributaries such as the Jane and Olga rivers, the Franklin is both delightful and scary. It hardly deserves the name of a whitewater river as its water is brandy-coloured, dyed by plant matter. After 125km (77 miles) the Franklin joins the Gordon River, which pours into Macquarie harbour on the southwest coast. Nowadays, rafting trips on the Franklin can last seven to 10 days. River-runners thrill to the rapids and the scenic beauty of this river, with

OPPOSITE: *The North Johnstone cuts a boulder-strewn course through the Great Dividing Range.*
LEFT: *The Upper Franklin River, once threatened by a hydroelectric scheme, is now safely conserved inside the Wild Rivers National Park.*

its inaccessible gorges and water containing no detergents, city sewage or heavy metals and chemicals from mines or factories upriver. New Zealand explorer and mountaineer Sir Edmund Hillary called this 'one of the last great wilderness areas in the world'.

However, it took a concerted public outcry against the mooted hydroelectric dams before the Franklin–Lower Gordon Wild Rivers National Park and World Heritage Site were declared in 1981. Campaigners were heavily involved in the federal elections of that year, an event that pushed conservation to the forefront of Australian politics for the first time.

It was not an easy fight. The local premier of Tasmania, Robin Grey, had been swept into office promising to boost job creation by building the hydro plants. A referendum showed that public opinion was evenly divided. But the environmental lobby would not let it rest there. They enlisted the support of the renowned British violinist, Sir Yehudi Menuhin, who passionately defended the river while attacking the destruction of Tasmania's tall eucalypt forests for wood-chipping. Only when the Australian prime minister, Bob Hawke, won a High Court judgement to intervene, was the future of the river fully secured.

WAIKATO RIVER, NORTH ISLAND, NEW ZEALAND

New Zealand's people, fondly known as Kiwis, are gregarious and always ready to extend a warm welcome and a cold beer to visitors. They are also afflicted by a compulsion to seek adventure – not surprising, surrounded as they are by the most awe-inspiring collection of natural assets in the form of mountains, beaches, caves and rivers. Self-reliance and modesty are national characteristics, reflected in the temperament of New Zealand's favourite son, Hillary. The man who conquered Everest in 1953 has remarked that he was just 'an ordinary bloke' who was lucky enough to get to climb mountain peaks.

These ordinary 'blokes' (including the female variety) today include scores of river-runners who test the limits of the extreme on their steep, gushing mountain creeks and waterfalls. As this was written, a party of kayakers with skills honed in their home country, were preparing to paddle the full length of the 1600km (960 miles) of the Antarctic Peninsula (really a set of islands joined by pack ice), braving temperatures of -20°C (0°F) in 'brash' ice – water like thick ice soup. A culture of outdoor adventure was hardly what their colonist predecessors envisaged when they settled New Zealand during the early and mid-19th century to become middle-class farmers and town artisans.

New Zealand's longest river, the Waikato (420km; 264 miles), has its headwaters at Mount Ruapehu in Tongariro National Park in the North Island. It has attracted the world's river-runners and is well known as a prime

OPPOSITE: *Rapidly flowing waters at the Huka Falls on the Waikato River, New Zealand present a challenge to paddlers from around the world.*
OPPOSITE: *Underground tubers, Waitomo Caves.*

CAVE TUBING AT WAITOMO CAVES

Floating down a river underground may not seem like everybody's idea of fun, but it is a hit with adventure travellers in the North Island, New Zealand. Every morning, curious 'moles' gather at the Black Water Café for a bagel and coffee, listening to the introduction to their tubing trip through the spectacular Ruakuri Cave, one of a network that forms part of the Waitomo Caves. It is hard to believe that hundreds of miles of tunnels wend their way under the gently rolling farm landscape. Local enthusiasts Peter Chandler and John Ash established what they called 'blackwater rafting' in 1987, so called because the underground streams run in the dark. The caves, about 210km (130 miles) south of Auckland, now attract about 400,000 visitors a year, of whom about 25,000 don a wetsuit and a caver's helmet to take the wet tour led by skilled guides.

Cave tubing is a curiosity in a country so well-endowed with whitewater rivers that no-one would ever need to feel cheated of special opportunities to go rafting. Yet the uniqueness of the experience is its own justification. The trip can feature an abseil (rappel) into the darkness and clambering down waterfalls. There is much splashing around in running water as one pushes along, half-sitting in an inner tube. One's easily visible white gumboots are used to fend off sharp projections. A headlamp picks out the stalactites adorning the ceiling. The New Zealand glow-worm, Arachnacampa luminosa, is the larva of a two-winged insect that emits light to attract food. Its display is magical.

These caves are part of a unique karst limestone landscape sculpted by water into blind valleys, sinkholes, springs, arches and fluted rock outcrops. In 1880, the discoverers called them a 'domain of beauty in forbidding darkness', finding hundreds of miles of labyrinthine tunnels, glow-worms and fluted chambers in a veritable lost world.

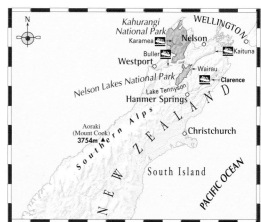

destination for jet-boating. After it leaves Lake Taupo, the name Waikato applies, meaning 'flowing water' in Maori, and though it has been dammed at no less than eight points, it strongly attracts paddlers (see panel on river rodeos, p69). Other luminaries have been drawn to it too: Queen Elizabeth II, Charles Lindbergh and James Michener have stayed over to see the Huka Falls.

The area around Lake Taupo in the volcanic Central Plateau, and the thermal region of Rotorua to its north, can be thought of as a southern terminus of the great Pacific Rim of Fire extending down the western Pacific from Tonga. The broad Huka Falls and nearby Aratiatia Rapids occur on a hard dyke across the softer lava rock. The falls themselves represent a special challenge to kayakers, first paddled in 1981 by New Zealander Greg Oke and his friend Nick Kerkham, and subsequently shot by many every year who respond with typical New Zealand flair to this challenge on their doorstep.

New Zealand boaters are great seekers of whitewater in every corner of the world. Yet all the river action anyone could want is to be found in their homeland. Conservation of New Zealand's rivers is a major concern of paddlers who fear that they will be destroyed by damming, quarrying and construction – a sobering thought, given the imagery of New Zealand as a gorgeous wilderness of water, rocks and snow in the blue South Pacific.

CLARENCE RIVER, SOUTH ISLAND

In the South Island, a profusion of energetic rivers pour off the Southern Alps, a chain of folded mountains which includes 17 that reach more than 3000m (9500ft). The highest is Aoraki/Mount Cook in the chilly south. Around the northern end of the island are the popular whitewater rivers, the Kaituna and Buller (Kawatiri) Rivers, both rising in the mountains of Nelson Lakes National Park, and the Karamea, winding through the superb wilderness of the Kahurangi National Park.

So many rivers could be mentioned it seems invidious to pick on just a few, but the Clarence River in the South Island is one of those special, accessible and beautiful waterways that make rafting and canoeing so popular as a form of recreation. The Clarence rises at Lake Tennyson, about 40km (24 miles) north of Hanmer Springs, and runs

ABOVE: *Float-rafting (drifting) down the Clarence River, with the Kaikoura ranges in the background.*
RIGHT: *The Roaring Lion rapid, on New Zealand's Karamea River, is a taxing run.*
FAR RIGHT: *Jet-boating on the Shotover River.*
FOLLOWING PAGES: *Aerated water at the bottom of a small drop, the Ariki Falls, hides a kayaker on New Zealand's Buller (Kawatiri) River, which rises in the mountains of Nelson Lakes National Park, South Island.*

between the Inland and Seaward Kaikoura ranges to reach the Pacific coastline. Rapids with bloodcurdling names like Jawbreaker, Carnage Corner and Sawtooth Gorge are big enough to be exciting but not enough to paralyze inexperienced paddlers with terror.

Although the river passes beneath the notable prominence of Mount Tapuaenuku (2885m; 9463ft), it is neither furiously fast nor brutally steep. The Clarence presents a combination of whitewater squeezing its way through a narrow gorge, and a relaxing float downriver.

JET-BOATING ON THE SHOTOVER LAUNCHES A CONTROVERSY

Jet-boating emerged in New Zealand when Bill Hamilton, a farmer, was looking for a means of transport on the swift, shallow rivers of the South Island. He devised an internal propeller (or impeller) to suck water through a chamber, then force it out through a flexible nozzle, giving the boat both direction and power. This was finalized in 1953, and by 1964 the first commercial trips were being run on the Shotover River near Queenstown, in the southern portion of the South Island, New Zealand.

Queenstown bills itself as the 'adventure capital of the world', which may not be far off the truth. Nestling beside Lake Wakatipu in the shadow of the Southern Alps, the compact town is an alpine resort with snow in winter, and hot and clear summers. In the area, bungee jumping takes place off the Pipeline Walkway, there are hikes to old gold workings at Arthur's Point and Skipper's Canyon, and aerial trips over the nearby Fiordland National Park.

Conventional rafting takes place on the Shotover and Kawarau rivers. Over one million visitors have jet-boated through the spectacular Shotover gorge. The 'Big Red' boats depart virtually hourly all year round, and big thrills await passengers. A highlight is a full 360-degree spin at full speed, bringing screams of exhilaration to everyone's lips.

The technology of jet-boating has spread worldwide, and jet-boat racing is now common on whitewater rivers. In the USA, park officials and environmental groups have attempted to limit whitewater powerboating to areas where the impact is minimized. Controversy has erupted over the intrusion of jet skis into such wilderness preserves as Canyonlands National Park, on the Colorado River. Here, rafters allege that the peace of the 300m-deep (1000ft) canyon has been disrupted by those driving noisy machines on the water, complete with what was described as a 'makeshift refuelling station'.

AFRICA

NILE * CONGO * ZAMBEZI * ORANGE * TUGELA

Former Colorado rafting guide turned adventure writer, Richard Bangs, set his personal stamp on the exploration of Africa when he opened up the Omo River in Ethiopia in 1973. The Omo rises in the same highlands that give birth to the Blue Nile, at Lake Tana, but then twists southwards towards Lake Turkana. For an American party without much experience of the Dark Continent, using the Library of Congress for their information was a limited form of preparation for the alien Omo with its hippopotamuses, African crocodiles, malaria and protozoan bowel infections. The magnificent surroundings reminded Bangs of the sheer rock abutments of Yosemite in California, but with many degrees of tropical heat – yet the presence of pitch-black, near-naked Suri villagers with enormous earrings and polished fighting sticks persuaded the rafters that they were not, after all, in familiar territory.

Bangs remarked that Africans loved to hear tales of far-off lands called California and America, while for his part he noted that he did not run rivers 'because they were there' but rather because they inspired him. Like the Westerners who had explored Africa's rivers before him – Mungo Park on the

Niger, James Bruce on the Blue Nile, Richard Burton and John Hanning Speke on the White Nile, Dr David Livingstone on the Zambezi and Henry Morton Stanley on the Congo – Bangs fell prey to the deep and lasting fascination for what was known as the Dark Continent but should rather have been dubbed the deep one.

With its assortment of humanity, colossal variety of landscapes, and amazing range of wildlife, all drawn to the huge but scarce water rivers, Africa remains largely an undiscovered paradise for river-runners. Wars and disease have kept visitors away, but especially in the more stable areas of Southern Africa, a strong rafting culture grew up in the final two decades of the 20th century.

In 1981, Bangs organized the first rafting descent of the feared Batoka Gorge on the Zambezi River, below Victoria Falls. Thanks to this initiative the Zambezi was soon to become Africa's hottest whitewater spot, concentrating a whole adventure industry around itself. In South Africa the Orange River in the red desert of the Kalahari/Namib and the Tugela River in lush central Zululand were pioneered, opening new gateways to the rivergods.

ABOVE, LEFT TO RIGHT: *Murchison falls on the Victoria Nile, Uganda; an aerial view of the island-studded Zambezi River, on the border between Zambia and Zimbabwe; the Orange River in the gorge below Augrabies Falls, South Africa.*
OPPOSITE: *Airborne over the drop, a kayaker launches off the lip of the Thrombosis Falls, Mzimkulu River, in KwaZulu-Natal, South Africa. The fall gets its name from the steep hike out.*

THE NILE, BURUNDI

A real-life Indiana Jones was the first to lead a canoe trip down the Nile – the world's longest river – from the source at Luvironza to the Mediterranean Sea. In 1955 adventurer extraordinaire, American John M Goddard, and two friends, Jean Laporte and Andre Davy, clambered up a 3m (10ft) pyramid at the ultimate source of the Nile in the Rift Valley region of what is today Burundi, and then set off in wood-and-canvas kayaks down the river of the pharoahs, Cleopatra, Lord Kitchener and John Hanning Speke. It was to be an odyssey of nine months, covering 6695km (4160 miles), which Goddard and his fellow adventurers survived in very good shape by avoiding crocodiles, and portaging around rapids and dams. They nearly starved, and right at the end of their trip they narrowly escaped death when set upon by a mob in the Nile delta. Only the intervention of three *gafirs* (village policemen) saved them, and *gafirs* were then kind enough to escort them on horseback all the way to the Mediterranean.

Goddard wrote about his trip in *National Geographic*. He did not mention that a first complete descent of the Nile was merely part of his total life's plan, which had many other ambitious objectives. At age 15 he had compiled a list of 127 'things to do' before he died. By the year 2000 he held a doctorate from a university in Utah, USA, was a popular motiva-

tional speaker, and to mark the Millennium, he wrote a book entitled *Survivor!* Goddard described residing with head-hunters in Borneo, milking poisonous snakes and much more, though he had to confess that at this point, with time running out, he had achieved only 108 of the items – and had not yet walked on the Moon!

The true source of the Nile was hotly debated by geographers for over 2000 years. Today, where the Nile drains from Lake Victoria, a plaque marks the spot where John Hanning Speke stood in 1862 and declared he had found the beginning of the river; and it is from near here that Nile whitewater rafting trips have been run in recent years. But in fact the most remote source, lying deep in southern Burundi, was only identified as late as 1937 by the German explorer Dr Burkhart Waldecker, who built the pyramid at the spring on the Luvironza River where Goddard and his friends began their trip a few years later.

The many names by which the river is known reveal its complex history. Starting as an upper branch of the Kagera River, the Nile flows from here for more than 500km (300 miles) via Rwanda and Tanzania into Uganda, before entering the northern portion of Lake Victoria. It leaves the lake as the Victoria Nile, then flows northwest across Uganda into Lake Albert (today known as Mobutu), after which it becomes the Albert Nile. Where Uganda shares its border with Sudan, the river takes on the name White Nile. At Khartoum,

Sudan's capital city, it is joined by its major tributary, the Blue Nile – which began its life as the Abbai, near Lake Tana in central Ethiopia – and together, simply as the Nile, the river embarks on its northbound journey to the Mediterranean.

Charismatic New Zealander Cam McLeay led the first rafting descent of the rapids of the Victoria Nile in 1966. As the river regularly carries 3000–4000 cumecs (more than 100,000–150,000cfs), the rapids in this section below Lake Victoria and above Lake Albert are huge. McLeay had done his homework before embarking on his trip. He knew that ancient Egyptian armies had explored the Nile up to and perhaps beyond the cataracts of Aswan; various colonial explorers had navigated large parts of the river; and in the early 1970s Sir Ranulph Fiennes, one of the greatest of modern explorers, proved the versatility of hovercraft by moving over land and water in the region of the middle Nile.

McLeay knew the steepest section of rapids between the Karuma and the Murchison falls had never been run. Boating was popular on the flat sections of the Victoria Nile, and tourists came to watch native Ugandans fishing by dugout canoe near the rapids, but no-one had thought of rafting trips. So he did it. In the course of an eight-day descent, his group counted 1400 hippos. They were charged every day by crocodiles, many of which were longer than the rafts and were the most aggressive he had seen in 20 years of boating on African rivers. The trip was nonetheless a great success and the Victoria Nile has won popular acclaim as an addition to the roster of top world whitewater destinations.

McLeay's company, Adrift, offered two-day trips on a 25km (16-mile) stretch with Grade 4 and 5 rapids. The trip started at Bujagali Falls in Uganda, with the rafts plunging down a wave train that led straight into Total Gunga, a juggernaut of big water. Lower down were Overtime, the Dead Dutchman, and Itanda. The latter is

riddled with holes big enough to swallow a bus and has only been paddled by a handful of kayakers whom colleagues regard as half-witted.

As the 21st century opened, the Bujagali Falls were scheduled for drowning. In 1998 the Ugandan government had confirmed its intention of building a dam on the rock dykes at Bujagali, though a year later the project seemed to be on hold for financial reasons. Nevertheless, the USA, busy decommissioning dams itself, urged Uganda to proceed for the sake of development, and the World Bank offered dam funding to the tune of US$460 million. Spokespersons for local NGOs, however, say that villagers and poor farmers have not been well informed and may not understand what is happening until too late.

THE BLUE NILE, ETHIOPIA

Whitewater there is aplenty on the Blue Nile in Ethiopia, but warfare and famine have made it virtually impossible to operate any kind of sustainable tourism venture. The Blue Nile issues quietly from the southeast corner of Lake Tana in lofty and rugged mountain country. This quiet progress does not persist; it flows over a lava dam to create the Tisisat Falls, and then charges northwest through hectic rapids to unite with the White Nile.

In the late 1960s and early 1970s respectively, two British groups rafted and kayaked the Blue Nile. In 1968 Emperor Haile Selassie of Ethiopia invited the British Army to make the first descent of the river, and a 60-strong rafting party was formed, led by Captain John Blashford-Snell of the Royal Engineers. Immense logistical problems presented themselves, not helped by the fact that high-grade rafting was in its infancy as far as the British Army was concerned. The imperial exploration was not an unmitigated success; large sections of the river were not run, and one man drowned.

The kayakers, mainly Briton Mike Jones and New Zealander Mick Hopkinson, who were later to make their names in the Himalayas, fared better, though they described themselves as 'young and brainless'. They passed the Tisisat Falls and reached the Shafartak bridge, covering a distance of 350km (220 miles) in all, during which they diced with bandits and fired off some 47 rounds at attacking crocodiles, from their collection of small arms. The whole experience left them in a state of numbness.

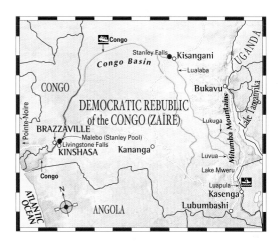

THE CONGO (ZAÏRE), CENTRAL AFRICA

The Congo (formerly known as the Zaïre) is the second longest river in Africa and provides the main transport route through the vast Central African basin. One could cover a distance of almost a third of the way around the earth's circumference just by following all the navigable channels and tributaries of this river, which form a web from east to west across the Democratic Republic of the Congo, as their main artery heads for the Atlantic Ocean. The tributaries total nearly 14,500km (9000 miles) of open water, and yet for all this, the Congo River can be a confusing maze. It has more than 4000 islands, mostly covered by dense vegetation, and its width can vary from 2 to 16km (1 to 10 miles) depending on how its many channels widen or constrict with seasonal rainfall.

While long stretches are placid, it is broken at intervals by huge rapids. The upper Congo begins in a series of lakes and descends through waterfalls and rapid-choked gorges. The middle section cascades down seven cataracts known as Boyoma Falls. In the lower section the river divides into two branches, forming the Malebo Pool at Kinshasa, then finally plunges over the Livingstone Falls. The falls and the Inga Rapids bar the river from being navigable from the West African coast.

Thousands of passengers wend their way on the jam-packed river boat from Kisangani in the east of the country to Kinshasa, the capital, in the southwest, with the thumping rhythm of the rhumba keeping up their spirits on the long, hot journey. They are mainly traders: crocodiles are pinioned in wooden frames, their mouths belted closed, being kept fresh for slaughter in Kinshasa where their skins and meat fetch a considerable price.

The matted jungles, walling off the river from the eyes of waterborne travellers, hide centuries of gloomy history and also harbour modern terrors like Ebola disease. (The

ABOVE: *Travel by water on the Congo River is faster and safer than by road in many areas of the Congo.*
OPPOSITE: *Traders, fishermen, soldiers and smugglers all thread the many-islanded channels of the river.*

Ebola River, a feeder stream of the Congo, is thought to be where the world's most deadly haemorrhagic fever originated some time around 1976.) Perhaps it is the very impenetrability and air of complete mystery that attracted early adventurers, driven by a variety of motives ranging from selfless Christianity to scientific curiosity, medical missionary work, and even the sporting instinct.

David Livingstone himself only penetrated the upper basin to the Lualaba River, a major headwater, never reaching the lower Congo. This feat was reserved for one of history's more controversial explorers, Henry Morton Stanley. Stanley's famous meeting with Livingstone on the shores of Lake Tanganyika – 'Dr Livingstone, I presume?' – has been described as the moment when a saintly philanthropist bumped into a journalistic adventurer, really the only thing in common being the English language. Stanley was the first to descend the Lualaba–Congo river system to its mouth in 1876 and 1877, establishing a navigable route to the interior which allowed the Congo to figure prominently in the colonization of Africa.

The first full traversing of the Congo River took place in 1974. A multi-specialist British team led by then Colonel John Blashford-Snell took four months to do the river, following in Stanley's footsteps. The expedition was no picnic: at one stage the party was spread over 1600km (995 miles) of jungle and river. Innovative jet boats with Ford V8 engines ran sections of the Livingstone Falls, some 32 cataracts which cover more than 320km (200 miles) between Kinshasa and the Atlantic. It was a fitting tribute to Livingstone himself, who had tried many kinds of river boat but never quite succeeded in conquering the Congo, the Shire (Malawi) or the Zambezi.

THE CONGO'S CHALLENGING TRIBUTARIES

Even in our own times, the Congo River and its tributaries offered a window onto Africa's treasures for a young South African paddler named Phil Lloyd and his friend Tony Hansen. Landing with their kayaks in 1987 at Lubumbashi in the extreme south of the country, near the border with Zambia, they were quickly overwhelmed by a country that was filled with hospitable people, and that was simultaneously beautiful, sad, awe-inspiring and puzzling. Together with two Belgian expatriates, they explored the Kafubu River running northwards and leading into the Luapula River, to near Kasenga. The rapids, fringed by thick jungle, were wide and often as long as 500m (550yd), culminating in the Johnstone Falls. One rapid, called Big Eyes, got its name from the fact that Hansen went over it backwards, upside down, but eventually successfully. Lloyd remarked that their trip dispelled many misconceptions about the Congo.

When they journeyed to the Kundelungu National Park below the Mitumba Mountains along the eastern border of the country, they found the pristine, red-rocked Lofoi River which drops 370m (1214ft) off the plateau at the Lakoba Falls. These are the second highest in Africa after the Tugela Falls but are seldom marked on maps. Hung with lianas and protected by the need for a considerable hike, the mountain river probably remains unrun as this is written, but after good rains, it would offer an Alpine-style creeking trip. It is one of thousands that are as yet unexplored in Africa's heart of white water. The Lofoi is a tributary of the Lufira and hence of the Lualaba, which in fact constitutes the upper reaches of the Congo River itself.

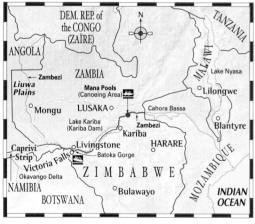

ZAMBEZI RIVER, ZIMBABWE

The Victoria Falls are the best-known geographical feature of Zambia and Zimbabwe, the two countries flanking the Zimbabwe River. With a maximum drop of 128m (420ft) and a width of 1.7km (1 mile), the falls form the biggest single curtain of falling water in the world.

Dr David Livingstone named the Victoria Falls in 1855 after Queen Victoria, but they have an older local name: Musi-oa-tunya, the 'smoke that thunders'. Plodding to the edge of the gorge, Livingstone beheld a thick rainforest that was perpetually watered by the steam rising from below. Birds flitted over the chasm.

Above the falls, the slow-moving river spreads across an immense channel dotted with islands where the cry of the fish eagle is heard.

'Scenes so lovely must have been gazed upon by angels in their flight', wrote Livingstone.

In the midst of the rainy season between January and June, the Victoria Falls live up to their name as the frightening thunder of some 8000 cumecs (290,000cfs) erupts over the chasm. Safe rafting and kayaking takes place between July and December when the flow is radically less, only about 1/25th of its high flow. The floods of 1958 sent nearly double the normal high-season flow over the falls, so that the earth could be felt shaking as distantly as a three-hour walk away.

Livingstone and others were wrong in their assumption that cataclysmic rifting of the earth's crust had created these falls. Much longer-term and indeed gentler processes have been involved. Over the ages, the river has cut backwards into soft basalt, forming the series of zigzags that constitute the 60km-long (37-mile) Batoka Gorge. The gorge sides mark the places where eight previous falls existed. The steep rapids are generally harder dykes that have resisted erosion.

Until about 11 million years ago, the upper Zambezi probably flowed southwards to join the Orange River in South Africa, but the earth warped and the river changed course. From its source in northern Zambia, the Zambezi loops into Angola then re-crosses Zambia, flowing southwards to Zimbabwe where it forms the northern border via Kariba Dam. From here it runs into Cabora Bassa in Mozambique, and finally meets the Indian Ocean. At 2740km (1700 miles) long, this puts the Zambezi just outside the world's top 30 longest rivers, pipped by number 30, the Para-Tocantas in South America at 2750km (1710 miles).

More than any other river, the Zambezi evokes the mystery and challenge of exploration, the mood of what was once called the Dark Continent. River-runners have come to know Africa as the continent of warm-water rivers, most of which remain beyond the ken of recreational

PRECEDING PAGES: *The vast channel across which the Zambezi River quietly flows, above the Falls.*
ABOVE AND RIGHT: *On crossing the lip of the Victoria Falls gorge, the river transforms into a mass of powerful thundering waters.*

boaters. The Zambezi is unusual in being relatively well known. It was first paddled from near its source to the sea by South African canoeists in 1957, without mishap as they avoided the major rapids. In 1981 the President of Zambia, Dr Kenneth Kaunda, agreed to allow American Richard Bangs and his outfit Sobek to tackle the Batoka. Their nine-day expedition succeeded, and the route to the Grand Canyon of Africa was open for business.

In 1985 rafting trips began in earnest, attracting so many travellers that Victoria Falls village and neighbouring Livingstone have since become the adrenaline centre of Africa. For three years, starting in 1995, the Camel Whitewater Challenge, unofficial world championship of rafting, took place on the Zambezi over eight rapids beginning at No. 4, a course of 10km (6 miles) taking about 50 minutes for the leaders. Many a raft flipped, leaving even the experienced raft crews gasping at the force of the water.

From the Boiling Pot, rafts spin into the current heading for a series of Grade 3–5 pool-and-drop thrillers including those with names like Morning Glory, Midnight Diner, Oblivion, Moemba Falls, Ghost Rider and many more. Oblivion (rapid No. 5) is said to flip more rafts than any rapid in the world, while Ghost Rider has the largest standing waves on the river. The crocodiles that plagued the Sobek rafting company seem mainly to have retired from the swift-water stretches, although boaters have been mauled by crocodiles and hippos above and below this zone.

Despite the mishaps experienced by some competitors, championships like the Camel Whitewater Challenge have heralded significant developments in competitive rafting. Paddlers meeting for the first time have been able to exchange ideas and trade safety knowhow. The International Rafting Federation (IRF) was born out of the cauldron of the Zambezi to set standards for training and assessment for commercial rafting, and it spurred the formation of several new national rafting bodies across the globe.

Visitors are often surprised that a strong tradition of boating exists among native paddlers, but it goes back a

RIGHT: *An oarboat filled with shrieking passengers dumps everyone in the Zambezi in yet another of the spectacular flips for which the river is famous.*

THE CROCODILE-INFESTED KUNENE

In 1965, South African Willem van Riet thought he had few illusions about the dangers of running the utterly remote Kunene River. He had read up on it and carefully studied the maps showing the river curling down out of Angola to form the border with Namibia (then South West Africa). He and Gordon Rowe – another pioneer of African rivers – agreed to kayak the river together. Drawn by the smell of adventure and determined to defy predictions of their early and certain deaths, the pair took off from a hamlet in Portuguese-ruled Angola on a 450km (280-mile) trip that nearly did end with their demise.

For the Kunene expedition, Rowe built specially strengthened fibreglass kayaks with fixed buoyancy. The boats were heavy, and without spraydecks they were often swamped in the unrelenting rapids of the Kunene, which dumped the men in the terrifying water. They bypassed two major falls, at Ruacana and Epupa along the Namibian border, but nearly came to grief on several smaller falls and in rapids choked by fallen boulders.

They felt hemmed in and trapped by the parched Baynes Mountains where peaks rose 1800m (5900ft) directly beside the river. Even today, very little is known about these mountains because history has passed them by. Angola's precious oil and diamond reserves lie further north. No roads or bridges cross the river in its lower 200km (125 miles), and for all practical purposes the Kunene is the river that time forgot. A few intrepid photographers and hikers have

penetrated the higher reaches of the Baynes near Epupa, but the depths of its gorges remain mysterious. Only the Namib's rare desert elephants make their pilgrimage to bathe in the Kunene and plunder its bankside greenery.

Van Riet carried a shotgun, and in the course of the three-week journey used it constantly to scare off voracious crocodiles, some as long as 5m (16ft). On one occasion, as they sped past a narrow stream, more than a dozen crocodiles launched themselves into the water in hot pursuit. It was often the rapids that saved them, for the crocodiles would retire to the pools from whence they came. The pair tried several times to hike out, but each time the appalling heat of the waterless Namib forced them to retreat back on the river. Having run out of food, and eaten virtually nothing for eight days, van Riet and Rowe finally reached the grim sandblown Skeleton Coast, and tottered up to a Portuguese police post. They were so weak they had to be carried into the police mess.

In 1995 van Riet revisited the Kunene with an expedition organized by Sobek, the American rafting company, and once again encountered the carnivorous reptiles. This time, the rafts travelled with a supply of rocks. When the reptiles appeared, the kayakers climbed aboard the rafts and pelted them with the local ammunition. It worked most of the time, but near the coast one of the rafts had its bow ripped completely off by one of the reptiles.

long way. Tribesmen fashion *mekoro* canoes from giant trees to fish the waters with basketwork traps and spears. In Barotseland, in the first half of each year, the Zambezi rises above its banks to soak the parched plains, and as it does so, the islands of the Lozi people of the flood plains are inundated. The Lozi then gather and cross, upriver of the rapids, on their annual journey known as the *Kuomboka*, to seek drier areas on the mainland, carrying their king, Litunga, in a grandly decorated barge poled along by 80 warriors in ceremonial dress.

If you take the 'Flight of Angels' in a fixed-wing helicopter or microlite over the Victoria Falls, you are likely to spot a rafting party or two setting off from the Boiling Pot below the falls. You may also glimpse someone taking the ultimate leap of faith – the 111m (364ft) bungee-jump off the railway bridge. Outdoor enthusiasts explore the bush country, but unfortunately this paradise is threatened by plans to dam the Batoka Gorge. This would drown virtually all the rapids up to No. 4, close to the foot of the falls. Only lack of finance prevented this from happening in the late 1990s, but mounting opposition and the lure of greater gains from ecotourism may prevent the dam being built at all.

THE ORANGE, SOUTH AFRICA

The African subcontinent is semi-arid, with most of the rain falling on South Africa's Drakensberg ('dragon mountains') and along the southeastern coastline. The Orange River starts on the rainswept heights of Lesotho, an independent kingdom falling within the confines of South Africa, then flows westwards across the latter into increasingly dry country. Measuring 2200km (1365 miles) from source to sea, it is almost as long as the Colorado (2333km; 1450 miles) in the USA. Its catchment is one-third larger than that of the Colorado, comprising nearly the whole of the central plateau of Southern Africa, including much of Botswana and Namibia. Torrential rains can produce floods of astonishing size. In 1988 the Orange was measured around 12,500 cumecs (441,000cfs), or about four times the size of the Colorado's highest flood in recent times. The Afrikaner Voortrekkers (pioneers) sometimes camped for weeks beside the river, waiting for its floods to subside before crossing it at well-known fords.

The Orange is one of the oldest rivers in the world. Imagine a watercourse so venerable it has worn away the landscape to reveal an Africa many times transformed from the earliest youth of our planet. A very stable granite shield, or basement rock, composed of the oldest of all known geological formations going back 3000 million years, appears at some of the rapids in the river's course.

FAR LEFT: *The remote and dangerous Kunene River, which forms the Angolan/Namibian border.*
ABOVE: *The folded strata of the gorge walls of the Orange rise dramatically above the river.*

In 1963, Willem van Riet (see panel opposite), an architectural student from Cape Town, South Africa, established his name in paddling circles with a lone 36-day descent of the Orange River. A friend pulled out of the trip early after nearly drowning in a whirlpool, so van Riet was forced to carry on alone.

The bleak Namib desert on the western coastline of Southern Africa, where the Orange River meets the Atlantic Ocean, is as lonely as the North and South Poles. Only the strange cactus-like plant *halfmens* – translated literally from the Afrikaans as 'half-man' – deludes one with the false promise of company. These spiny succulents, topped with tufts of

leaves like hair, stand on rock outcrops and are thought by the Khoi people to be charmed human beings ready to mesmerize travellers in the friendless barren desert.

Augrabies waterfall in the lower Kalahari Desert, just before the Orange forms its boundary between Namibia and South Africa, comprises 19 separate falls with one direct drop of 145m (476ft). At high flows the volume going over the falls can exceed that of the better known Victoria Falls on the Zambezi. Just above Augrabies is a rafting day-trip where visitors may be lucky to spot rhinoceros and gemsbok.

In 1999, the Camel Whitewater Challenge was held in the depths of the Augrabies gorge by special dispensation of the National Parks authority, as the gorge is normally closed to all boaters.

Below the Augrabies waterfall, at the Onseepkans gorge, the river splits into what is known as 'Big George', a mischievous trench filled with potholes and graded 4–5, and 'Little George', or the chicken run. This arm, graded 2–3, runs around an island, then crashes over the 40m (130ft) Gariep Falls into a furious boiling pot where the channels meet. Both are kayaked and rafted.

THE TUGELA, SOUTH AFRICA

The Tugela rises in virtually the same place as the Orange, atop Mont Aux Sources in the high Drakensberg. Beginning as a pencil-thin streamlet seeping from a marsh above the winter snowline, it suddenly slips over the edge of the escarpment to fall directly to the foothills of the range. At 948m (3109ft) the Tugela Falls are the world's second highest after the Angel Falls in Venezuela (South America), which measure 979m (3212ft). Known by the Zulus as Uthukela – 'the one that startles' – the Tugela has been the site of many battles involving tribal people, British colonial armies, Boer commandos, freedom fighters, and lately gun-runners, drug-dealers and security forces. It is a river of conflict.

The region through which it runs was once ruled by the fearsome king, Shaka. Around 1808 he inherited the chieftainship of a then minor tribe known as the Zulus and proceeded to turn it into the mightiest military machine Africa had ever seen. Shaka's *impis* (armies), equipped with short stabbing spears called *assegais* and shields of rawhide skins, subdued all surrounding tribes and drove thousands of refugees into the interior and northwards into Africa as far as present-day Malawi. There are echoes of the powerful Zulu era in the performances of wildly energetic Zulu dancers who today entertain raft groups around the campfire on humid summer nights.

OPPOSITE: *A view across the falls from the Augrabies Falls National Park in Namibia.*
LEFT: *Although the Tugela begins its life as a wispy rivulet, flooding tributaries can swell the river's waters to a torrential mass in its lower reaches.*

The first of the Tugela gorges is a cleft in the foot of the Drakensberg, shot only by extreme kayakers and then only after heavy rains have turned the mountain stream into a roaring torrent. Caves in the surrounding countryside contain exquisite animal paintings left by the San (Bushmen) people on the exposed horizontal strata of light yellow to grey sandstone. The overhangs invariably face somewhere between north and east because Bushmen believe that the 'good' god lives in the east, and the 'evil' god in the west. The earliest known paintings in Southern Africa are 27,000 years old, although in the Tugela region they are probably no more than 4000 to a few hundred years old. They depict hunting scenes, ritual dancing, and the arrival of the first black agricultural tribes, and later, white settlers.

Tributaries swell the Tugela River as it crosses the grassy Natal Midlands, so by the time it reaches the town of Colenso, it is a muscular brown channel ready to assert its power. Whitewater rafting begins here in earnest, at the lip of the Tugela Canyon. This is the first of four major gorges on the river's final 300km (186-mile) run to the Indian Ocean. The Canyon, the Red Ravine, the Tugela Gorge and finally the Little Gorge are the product of deep downcutting by a young river as the land has tilted and risen around it during recent geological times. When it floods, the gorge is a nightmare of thundering water almost black from the erosion of basalt-rich soils.

Near the mouth of the river is the Ultimatum Tree where in 1879 Britain warned the Zulu nation to accept indirect rule or be conquered. In keeping with the character of the Tugela, this brash warning led only to the defeat of the British themselves, who were routed at the battle of Isandhlwana. Although the Zulu nation was finally subdued by the sledgehammer of colonialism, the Tugela remained a boundary between black and white. Today, black and white river guides work together on the river, as free and equal countrymen of the democracy established in 1994.

LEFT: *Slipping off the edge of the Drakensberg escarpment, the Tugela Falls are the world's second highest after Venezuela's Angel Falls.*
RIGHT: *Competitors in the Duzi race, held annually in KwaZulu-Natal, South Africa.*

THE DUZI

In South Africa's eastern province of KwaZulu-Natal, rivers rise then run in steep channels to the sea, with the only flat land lying high above them. The Mkomazi ('place of cows') is one of these rivers, as is the Mzimkulu ('the great one'), and the Mzimvubu ('place of the hippopotamus').

After World War II, a group of young conservationists discovered that the remains of primitive Africa could be found in the deep gorges of these rivers. Wildlife still lurked there: bushbuck, otters, even the odd crocodile. Tribal peoples lived on the slopes in grass huts, avoiding temperature inversion by siting their homesteads halfway up the mountainsides – where they could also keep a good lookout for enemies.

In 1951 eight men, including Ian Player of the Natal Parks Board, set off on one of the world's first river endurance races, the Duzi (an anglicized version of the Zulu name, Msindusi). Paddling a tin canoe down Duzi stream into the Mgeni River, it took Player six gruelling days to get from the small town of Pietermaritzburg to the city of Durban, on the east coast.

The first trip down these two rivers had been made as long ago as 1893 by local men William Foley and Paul Marianny, but Player started a phenomenon. The Duzi Marathon has become an institutionalized canoeing ordeal over three days in July every year, attracting over 1000 hardy male and female competitors to the muggy hills of KwaZulu-Natal.

GLOSSARY

ARTIFICIAL RIVER A man-made stream of water flowing in a channel designed for a specific purpose, such as whitewater sport.

BIG WATER High-volume rapids packing immense power.

BOILING WATER Very turbulent water gushing up from the depths is said to be boiling; another term for it is 'squirrily'.

BOULDER SIEVE Large rocks strewn across a rapid are a garden, and become a boulder sieve if they are close together.

BRAIDED Shallow channels flowing between rocks, sand banks or vegetation.

CFS Cubic feet per second, sometimes referred to as second/feet; the imperial measurement for the volume of water flowing per second past any given point in the channel. 100 cfs equals 2.83 cubic metres per second (cumecs), see cumecs.

CHUTE A narrow passage in a river where the current speeds up and its energy is amplified.

CLASS See grade.

CUMECS Cubic metres per second, often written m^3. This is the metric measurement for the volume of water flowing per second past any given point in the channel. One cubic metre (cumec) equals 35.287 cubic feet per second (cfs), see cfs.

DECLIVITY A steady downward inclination or slope of the river, causing the water to speed up.

EDDY Water that is still, slow-moving, or moving upstream behind an obstacle amid moving currents.

EXTREME BOATING Any form of kayaking, rafting or use of a watercraft in high-grade rapids. This includes running waterfalls and Grade 5 & 6 rapids. Injury and drowning are possible.

FLATWATER When river currents are hardly moving or have little gradient they are regarded as flatwater.

FLUME An artificial channel or narrow chute in a river, often ending in a spout of water.

GALLOWAY POSITION Named after oarboater Nathaniel Galloway more than a century ago, this is the basic position for steering down rapids. The oarsman faces ahead rather than with his back to the bows.

GRADE Rapids are graded or classed according to their level of difficulty and danger. The international system uses 1 (moving water that is easy and straightforward) to 6 (the limit of difficulty and usually regarded as unrunnable and likely to be fatal). An alternative 1–10 grading treats 10 as the extreme of difficulty (see Safety on Rivers and Grading Table on p00).

GRADIENT The steepness or angle of the river as it flows downhill. Gradient is normally measured in feet per mile because the metric measurement is awkward.

HAIRBOATER/HAIRBALL BOATER A paddler who runs truly wild rapids. The term may originate from the spray coming off the waves, giving the appearance of hair.

HOLE (OR HYDRAULIC) Water plunging over an obstacle will reverse on itself. The effect is that both the current from upstream and the reversal from downstream flow into the hole. The hydraulic effect keeps boats and swimmers in the hole.

KARST See travertine and tufa.

KEEPER A hole or reversal whose suck-back is so powerful that it will keep any boat or swimmers indefinitely. See hole.

LATERALS Diagonal waves peeling off a cliff or narrow bank, and indicating a converging force.

LOAD The amount of sediment, e.g. glacial grit or eroded soil, carried in a body of moving water.

OARBOAT Any river boat that is powered and/or steered by an oarsman. Rowing on rivers is unusual in that the oarsman usally faces forward, pushing rather than pulling the oars in what is known as the portegee stroke. See Galloway position.

PADDLECAT A twin-hulled inflatable catamaran where the paddlers kneel or sit on the pontoons.

POOL-AND-DROP The rapids consist of chutes and boulder gardens separated by calmer water. See staircase.

POUROVER A current going over a rock or other river feature, creating a hump in the water, often with a hole downstream of it. See hole.

PUT-IN The place on the river where a trip starts.

RIVER LEFT AND RIGHT Left and right on the river when the paddler is looking downstream.

RIVER-RUNNING The activity of moving downriver, for pleasure or some other purpose, using any kind of boat to navigate through rapids.

RODEO Freestyle playboating in holes and powerful currents. Paddlers in kayaks, canoes and rafts execute moves for points.

SCOUT To scout is to survey the rapid from the bank or from the water. Entire parties can scout rapids, but a scout is often the term used to describe the boater in front of the group.

SCOW A flat-bottomed river boat with sweep oars at bow and stern to steer through channels.

SLALOM KAYAKING An Olympic sport, this involves paddling through gates hung over a rapid, scoring points for speed and losing points if the gates are touched or missed.

SPRAYDECK The sealing skirt worn by a kayaker around the midriff and attached to the cockpit coaming.

STAIRCASE Continuous cascading rapids without respite, only the eddies allowing pause.

STOPPER A wall of water across the river, caused by an underwater ledge or sudden drop. The foam pile of a stopper stops boats and may keep them there. It is fun to surf a manageable stopper.

STRAINER OR SIEVE Any obstacle through which the current can flow while boats or people are stopped, e.g. tree branches or narrow rocky clefts.

SWIMMER A person who falls out of a boat involuntarily and may need rescue.

TAKE-OUT The place on the river where the trip ends. See put-in.

TRAVERTINE/TUFA A porous rock with a spongy appearance formed by deposits of calcium carbonate or limestone.

WAVE TRAIN Standing waves in a sequence that remains fairly predictable.

WILDWATER Turbulent, heavily aerated water in rapids.

Z-PULLEY OR Z-DRAG A roping system using the mechanical advantage of exerting greater haul on a line with the aim of freeing a boat stuck on rocks.

REFERENCES AND FURTHER READING

Addison, Corran (1998) **Kayaker's Little Book of Wisdom.** ICS Books, Merriville, Illinois.

Addison, Graeme (2000) **Adventure Sport Series: Whitewater Rafting.** New Holland Publishers, London.

Bangs, Richard & Kallen, Christian (1989) **Riding the Dragon's Back: the race to raft the upper Yangtze.** Dell Publishing (Bantam Doubleday Dell), New York.

Bangs, Richard & Kallen, Christian (1985) **Rivergods: exploring the world's great wild rivers.** Sierra Club Books, San Francisco.

Bennett, Jeff (ed) (1992) **Class Five Chronicles: Things Mother Never Told You 'Bout Whitewater.** Swiftwater Publishing Company, Portland, Oregon.

Chamoli, S P (1992) **Rafting down the Mystic Brahmaputra.** Vikas Publishing House.

Charles, Graham (1999) **New Zealand Whitewater: 120 great kayaking runs.** Craig Potton Publishing, Nelson, New Zealand.

Connolly, Bob (1981) **The Fight for the Franklin: the story of Australia's last wild river.** Cassell Australia, North Melbourne, Victoria.

Ferraro, Franco (1998) **White Water Safety and Rescue.** Pesda Press, Wales.

Gavrilov, Vladimir (1997) **Rivers of an Unknown Land.** Raftweb http://www.raft.org/ (INTERNET BOOK)

Glück, Nelson (1946) **The River Jordan: an illustrated account of the earth's most storied river.** The Jewish Publication Society of America. Philadelphia.

Guilar, Liam (1998) **Dancing with the Bear.** Idaho State University Outdoor Program http://www.isu.edu/outdoor/ (INTERNET BOOK)

Jones, Mike (1979) **Canoeing Down Everest.** Mike Jones Films/Chameleon Press, West Yorkshire & London.

Kane, Joe (1990) **Running the Amazon.** Vintage Departures (Random House), New York.

Knowles, Peter (1999) **Whitewater Nepal: a rivers guidebook for kayakers and rafters.** Rivers Publishing UK, Leicester.

Main, Michael (1990) **Zambezi: Journey of a River.** Southern Books, Halfway House, South Africa.

Manby, Dave (ed) (1999) **Many Rivers to Run.** Coruh River Press, Colchester, Essex.

McCully, Patrick (1996) **Silenced Rivers: The ecology and politics of large dams.** Zed Books, London.

Moorehead, Alan (1960) **The White Nile.** Hamish Hamilton, London.

Moorehead, Alan (1962) **The Blue Nile.** Hamish Hamilton, London.

Nicolson, Nigel (1975) **The Himalayas: the World's Wild Places.** Time-Life Books, Amsterdam.

O'Hanlon, Redmond (1996) **Congo Journey.** Hamish Hamilton, London.

Peissel, Michel (1974) **The Great Himalayan Passage: Adventure Extraordinary by Hovercraft.** Collins, London.

Player, Ian (1964) **Men, Rivers and Canoes.** Simondium Publishers, Cape Town.

Pelton, Robert Young (1998) **The World's Most Dangerous Places.** Fielding Worldwide Inc, Redondo Beach, California.

Sedivy, Bill (1995) **Rivers End: a Collection of Bedtime Stories for Paddlers.** Big Dog Publications, Newbury, Ohio.

Shoumatoff, Alex (1988) **In Southern Light: Trekking through Zaire and the Amazon.** Corgi Books, London.

Sterling, Tom (1973) **The Amazon: The World's Wild Places.** Time-Life, Amsterdam.

Teal, Louise (1994) **Breaking into the Current: boatwomen of the Grand Canyon.** University of Arizona Press. Arizona.

Walbridge, Charles & Sundmacher, Wayne A Snr (1995) **Whitewater Rescue Manual: new techniques for canoeists, kayakers, and rafters.** Ragged Mountain Press, Camden, Maine.

Wallach, Jeff (1996) **What the River Says: whitewater journeys along the inner frontier.** Blue Heron Publishing, Hillsboro, Oregon.

Watters, Ron (1994) **Never Turn Back: the life of whitewater pioneer Walt Blackadar.** Great Rift Press, Pocatello, Idaho.

Welch, Vince; Conley, Cort; and Dimock, Brad (1998) **The Doing of the Thing: the brief brilliant whitewater career of Buzz Holmstrom.** Fretwater Press, Arizona.

Winchester, Simon (1996) **The River at the Centre of the World: a journey up the Yangtze and back in Chinese time.** Penguin, London.

Wood, Robert S (1984) **Whitewater Boatman: the making of a river guide,** Ten Speed Press, Berkeley, California.

INDEX

Page numbers in bold denote photographs

Abbey, Edward 43
Addison, Corran 22, 31
Alas River **124**, 125
Aldeyjarfoss (falls) 31, 68
Alexander, Michael 106
Alsek River 19, 20, **26**, 29
Amazon River 14, 18, 46, 50–54
American River 16, 36–37, **37**
Angara River 94
Angel Falls 58, **58**
Apurimac River 51, **51**
Aratiatia Rapids 134
Ariki Falls **136–137**
Arkansas River 4
Ash, John 133
Augrabies Falls 151, **152**
Aulick, R 88
Baghirathi River 4
Baker, Guy 89
Baker, Ian 120
Baker, Shaun 31, 68
Bangs, Richard 20, 23, 24, 102, 138, 148
Barron River 130
Batoka Gorge 138, 146, 150
Beer, Bill 42
Berman, Tao 31
Bhote Kosi River **110–111**
Big Eyes rapid 142
Biggs, Tim 51
Bío-Bío River 21, 46, 57, **57**
Black Canyon 1
Blackadar, Walt 20, 21, 30
Blashford-Snell, John 19, 128, 141, 142
Blomqvist, Anders 72
Boyoma Falls 142
Brahmaputra River 120
Braldu River 112–116, **112**, **113**
Bristow, Scott 44, **44**
Bujagali Falls 140, 141
Buller River **136–137**
Burg, Amos 18
Burns, Arlene 22, 121
canyon
   Cataract 39, 41, 42
   Chocolate (Norway) **67**
   Colca River (Peru) 60–62
   Devil's 21
   Fish River (Namibia) 14, **14**
   Glenwood 41
   Gore 41
   Grand (USA) 14, **14**, 16, **16**, 17, **19**, 26
   Imst 76
   Inferno 55
   Skippers **122**
   Tekeze 23
   Tugela 154
   Turnback 30
   Upper Gorge 42
Caroni River 58
Carroll, Shannon 24, 31
Cartier, Jacques 28

Casiquiare Canal 56, 58
Cataract Canyon 39, 41, 42
Chamberlain Falls 37
Chamoli, 'SP' 121
Chandler, Peter 133
Chassing, Nico 24
Chatkal River 95, **98–99**
Chilli Bar 37
Chmielinski, Piotr 51, 53
Chocolate Canyon 67
Churchill Falls 28
Churchill River see Mishta-Shipu River
Chuya River 92, **93**
Chuya River rally 23
Ciroteau, François 22
Clarence River 134–135, **134**
Clark, William 34
Cockerell, Christopher 19
Colca River 46
Colca River Canyon 60–62
Colorado River 6, 14, **14**, **15**, 19, 26, 27,
   32–33, 38–43, **39**, **40**
Congo River 142, **143**
Coruh River 87, **87**
Coyne, Mick 69
Crantz, David 17
Daggett, John 42
Dalton, Jack 17
Davy, Andre 140
Day, Horace 16, 34
De Coronado, Francisco Vasquez 42
Dettifoss 68
Devil's Canyon 21
Devil's Creek rapid 30
Dez River **88**, 89
Dixon, Dan 22, 121
Dragon's Teeth Rapid 103
Dudh Kosi River 21, 108
Duzi Marathon 18, 155, **155**
Earth River Expeditions 62
Eastwood, Trevor 76
El Wasto rapid **105**
Ellard, Allan 117
Epupa Falls 150
Euphrates River 14, 17, 87
falls 19
   Aldeyjarfoss 31, 68
   Angel 58, **58**
   Asiki **136–137**
   Augrabies 151, **152**
   Boyoma 142
   Bujagali 140, 141
   Chamberlain 37
   Churchill 28
   Dettifoss 68
   Epupa 150
   Gariep 151
   Háifoss 68
   Hidden 121
   Huka **132**, 134
   Johnson Creek 31
   Johnstone 142
   Kootenai 21

Lakoba 142
Livingstone 142
Murchison **138**
Niagara 19
Ruacana 150
Sahalie 24, 31
Seven Teacups 63
Thrombosis **139**
Tignes 22, 31
Tisisat **141**
Tugela 153, **154**
Ula **66**, 72
Urrum **74–75**
Victoria 16, 19, 151
Faukstad Hole 73, **73**
Ferchenkar Glacier 91
Fish River Canyon 14, **14**
Fisher, Steve 24
Five Falls rapids 21
Foley, William 155
Franklin River 130, 131–132, **131**
Fraser, Morna 62
freestyle
   competitions 69
   kayaking 23
   rodeo 69
Fremont, John 16, 34
Fulljames Rapids 69
Futaleufu River **47**, 55, 64–65
Galloway, Nathaniel 17
Gariep Falls 151
Gates of Inferno rapid 55
Gavrilov, Vladimir 37, 93
Ghiglieri, Michael 125
Giant Gap 36
Giddings, J Calvin 51
Gilgit River **90**
Glave, Edward James 17
Glenwood Canyon 41
Goddard, John M 18, 140
Gore Canyon 41
Gorge 37
Grand Canyon 14, **14**, 16, **16**, 17, **19**, 26
Great Bend (Yangtze River) 102
Guilar, Liam 95
Gunnison River 1, 20, 42
Hacienda Canco 61
Háifoss 68
Hamilton, Bill 135
Hansen, Tony 23, 142
Hatch, Bus 18
Hell's Gate 21
Hertz, Eric 62, 64
Heyerdahl, Thor 17
Hidden Falls 121
Holmstrom, Buzz 42
Hooker River **123**
Hopkinson, Mick 108, 116, 141
Horn, Mike 52–54, 60
hovercraft 19
Huka Falls **132**, 134
Hutiao Shoal 102
hydrospeed 52

Imst Canyon 76
Indus River **14**, 18, 19, 21, 23, **116**
Inferno Canyon 55
Inn River 76–78
International Rafting Federation (IRF) 148
International Rivers Network (IRN) 103
Isere River 23
jet-boating 135, **135**
Johnson Creek 31
Johnstone Falls 142
Johnstone River 130, **130**
Jökulsá á Fjöllum River 68, **68**
Jones, Mike 20, 21, 24, 58, 76, 108, 112, 141
Jordan River 16, 17, 86–89
Kaituna River **122**
Kali Gandaki River **104**, 106–108
Kane, Joe 51, 62
Karamea River **122**
Karnali River **104**
Katun River 92, **92**
Kaweah River 36, **36**
kayak
   folding 80
   plastic 20
Kelemen, Zeljko 83
Kellner, Jan 23
Kerkham, Nick 134
Klepper boat 80
Klepper, Johannes 17, 80
Kon-Tiki 17
Kootenai Falls 21
Kootenai River 21
Kunene River 19, 150, **150**
Lake Baikal 94, **94**
Lakoba Falls 142
Laporte, Jean 140
Lava Falls Rapid **32–33**
Lee, Katie 43
Lesser, Rob 21
Lewis, Meriwether 34
Lindgren, Scott 24
Litton, Martin 17, 19
Livingstone Falls 142
Livingstone, Dr David 16, 142, 146
Lloyd, Phil 23, 142
Lofoi Falls 142
Loomis, Doc 93
Luapula River 23
Lynch, Lieut John 16
Lynch, Lieut William F 88
MacGregor, John 16, 17, 80
Mae Taeng River 124
Maipure Rapids 58
Manby, Dave 87, 112, 116
Maoshu, Yao 102
maps
   Alaska 28
   Arizona 37
   Australia 130
   Austria 76
   Balkans 81
   Brazil 51
   California 36

Canada 28
Chile 64
China 101
Costa Rica 49
Himalayas 106
Iceland 68
Idaho 34
India 117
Indonesia 125
Iran 89
Kyrgyzstan 95
Middle East 87
New Zealand 134
Norway 72
Orange River 151
Papua New Guinea 127
Peru 60
Siberia 92
Switzerland 76
Tasmania 131
Tennessee 43
Venezuela 56
World 10-11
Zimbabwe 146
Marianny, Paul 155
Marsyandi River 24
Mazhoy Cascades 92, **93**
McGinnis, Bill 72
McKenzie drift boat 18
McLeay, Cam 23, 140
Mekong River 23
Mendes, Chico 50
Merchant, Bob 89
Misahualli River **59**
Mishta-Shipu River 28
Moksu River **114-115**
Mreznica River 81, **81**, 83
Murchison Falls **138**
Murray River 130
Musi-oa-Tunya see Victoria Falls
Napo River 54
Nepean River 131, **131**
Nepean whitewater course 131
Nevills, Norman 18
New River 45, **45**
Niagara Falls 19
Nigardselva River **66**
Niger River 14
Nile 14, 17, **140-141**, **140**
Albert 140
Blue 19, 140, 141
Victoria 140
White 140
No. 1 rapid (Zambezi) 22
No. 2 rapid (Zambezi) 22
No. 4 rapid (Zambezi) 148
No. 7 rapid (Zambezi) **7**
North Johnstone River 23
Ocoee River 23, 43-45, **43**
Oke, Greg 134
Omo River 20, 138
Orange River 138, **138**, 150-151, **151**
Orinoco River 19, 56-58, **56**

Ötz River 76, **76**
Pacuare River **48**, 49
Padas River 127, **127**
paddlecat raft 93, **96, 97**
Pai River 124, **124**
Peissel, Michel 20, 106
Peralta rapids 49
Pierrepont, Holme 22
Pjörsá River 68
Platte River 16
Player, Ian 18, 155
plohts 93
Potomac River 44, **44**
Powell, John Wesley 16, 41-42
Project Raft 23, 93
Pskem River **90**, 95, **96, 97**
rapids 19
  All Day's Sucker (Chatkal River) 95
  artificial 20, 23, 24, 131
  Big Eyes 142
  Big George (Orange River) 151
  Binary Proposition (Chatkal River) 95, **98-99**
  Boiling Pot (Zambezi River) 148
  Carnage Corner (Clarence River) 135
  Chilli Bar (American River) 37
  Devil's Creek 30
  Dragon's Teeth (Mekong River) 103
  El Wasto (Sun Kosi River) **105**
  Five Falls 21
  Fulljames (Waikato River) 69
  Gates of Inferno 55
  Gatsien (Vaal River) 69
  Ghost Rider (Zambezi River) 148
  Giant Gap (American River) 36
  grading system 13
  Granite (Colorado River) 38
  Gulf Stream (Sjoa River) 72
  Hance (Colorado River) 38
  Haystack (Salmon River) 34
  Hell's Kitchen (Tuolumne River) 37
  Himalaya (Futaleufu River) 64
  Horn Creek (Colorado River) 38
  House Rock (Salmon River) 34
  Inferno Canyon (Futaleufu River) 64
  Jawbreaker (Clarence River) 135
  Khyber Pass (Futaleufu River) 64
  Lava Falls **32-33**, 38
  Liangjiarien (Yangtze River) 102
  Little George (Orange River) 151
  Lost Yak (Bío-Bío River) 57
  Maipure (Amazon River) 58
  Mantianxing (Yangtze River) 102
  Marble Creek (Salmon River) 34
  Midnight Diner (Zambezi River) 148
  Moemba Falls (Zambezi River) 148
  Morning Glory (Zambezi River) 148
  Nemesis (Tuolumne River) 37
  No. 1 (Zambezi) 22
  No. 2 (Zambezi) 22
  No. 4 (Zambezi) 148
  No. 7 (Zambezi) **7**
  Oblivion (Zambezi River) 148
  Peralta (Reventazon River) 49

Pinball (Tuolumne River) 37
Praesidium (Chuya River) 92
Rapids of Death 58
Roaring Lion 134
Sawtooth Gorge (Clarence River) 135
Seti Beni (Kali Gandaki River) **107**
Soc'em Dog 21
Tappen Falls (Salmon River) 34
Terminator (Futaleufu River) 64
Thread-the-Needle (Tuolumne River) 37
Throne Room (Futaleufu River) 64
Toothache (Apurimac River) 51
Tunnel Chute (American River) 37
Your First and Last Laugh (Apurimac River) 51
Zeta (Futaleufu River) 64
Red Zone 54
Reventazon River 49
RhaniGat palace ruins 106
Rhondu Gorges **14**, 23, **116**
Rio Claro (Chile) 63
Río Misahualli (Ecuador) 54, **65**
rivers, mythology of 121
Roaring Lion Rapid **134**
Rob Roy 80
Rowe, Gordon 19, 150
Ruacana Falls 150
Ruakuri Cave 133
safety and survival 24
Sahalie Falls 24, 31
Sakharov, Andrei 94
Salmon River 18, **34**, 34
Salween River 103, **103**
Sangkhalia River 124
Seti Beni rapid **107**
Seven Teacups 63
Shotover River 135
Shotover River Valley **122**
Sjoa River 67, **70-71**, 73
Skippers Canyon **122**
Skjálfandafljót River 68
Skykomish River **2-3**
slalom course 44
Smokjanovic, Milka 83
Sobek company 20, 21, 22, 102, 148, 150
Soc'em Dog rapids 21
Soca River 66, **82**, 83, **84-85**
Speke, John Hanning 16, 140
Stanley, Henry Morton 17, 142
Starkell, Don and Dana 56, 58
Stone, Julius 17
Stone, Steve 54
Stormy River 91
Strickland River 128, 129
Sun Kosi River 20, 21, **104**, 105, 108, **108-109**, 121
Sutlej River 117, **117**
Syr Darya River 95
Tamur River 22-23, 117
tankwa 17
Tatshenshini River 17, **26**, 28, **30-31**
Team Gorky 94
Teesta River 117

Tekeze Canyon 23
rafting 124
Thomas, Lowell 19
Three Gorges Dam 103
Thrombosis Falls **139**
Tiger Leaping Gorge 102
Tignes Falls 22, 31
Tigris River 14, 17, 87
Tisisat Falls **141**
Tongass National Forest 29
Trisuli River 108
Truran, Jerome 62
Tsangpo River 22, 120, **120**
Tugela Canyon 154
Tugela Falls 153, **154**
Tugela River 138, 153-155, **153**
Tully River 130
Tunnel Chute Rapid 37
Tuolumne River 22, **26**, 37, **37**
Turnback Canyon 30
Ula Falls 66, 72
Umsindusi River 18
Upper Gorge Canyon 42
Urrum Fall **74-75**
Urubamba River **46**
US Whitewater Accident Report 54
Van Riet, Willem 19, 37, 150, 151
Vander-Molen, Paul 69
Victoria Falls 16, 19, 151
  Batoka Gorge **146, 147**
Von Moltke, Count Helmuth 17
Waikato River **132**, 133
Waitomo Caves 133, **133**
Waldecker, Dr Burkhart 140
Warren, Ken 102
White, Georgie 42
White, James 16
whitewater boats, development of 17
whitewater events
  Camel Whitewater Challenge 48, 49, 64, 148, 151
  Chuya Rally 92, 94
  Duzi Marathon 18
  Last Tanga in Parys 69
  Sjoa Kayak Festival 72
  World Rodeo Championships 69
whitewater river boating, development of 16-24
Whiting, John D 18, 89
Whitmore, Bryce 19
Wilde, John 21, 108
Winn, Peter 23, 103
Yangtze River 14, 22, **90**, **100**, **101**, 102-103
Yost, John 20, 102
Zambezi River 16, 138, **138**, **144-145**, 146-150
Ziller River 76

PHOTOGRAPHIC CREDITS

Key to photographers (copyright rests with photographers and/or their agents as listed below)

GA = Graeme Addison; DA = David Allardice; Ax = Axiom; GB = Guy Bakers; AB = Andy Belcher; ABl = Anders Blomqvist; DB = Dugald Bremner; TB = Tim Brown; ZB = Zbigniew Bzdak; JC = John Cleare; GC = Gerald Cubitt; DD = David Daboll; B&BD = Bruce & Barbara Duncan; PD = Paul Dymond; DE = David Edwards; AE = Allan Ellard; LF = Lee Farrant; AF = Alan Fox; GI = Gallo Images; GI/TS = Gallo Images/Tony Stone Images; IG = Itamar Grinberg; LG = Liam Guilar; DH = Dunbar Hardy; AH = Al Harvey; BH = Bill Hatcher; HL = Hutchison Library; JJ = Jack Jackson; JK = Julie Kelter; AK = Anja Klotz; OK = Oleg Kosterin; FM = Dr Franz Memelauer; NG = National Geographic magazine; MN = Michael Neuman; KOB = Kevin O'Brien; PPL/PB = PPL/Peter Bentley; MS = Mark Silburn; SAP/TM = South American Pictures/Tony Morrison; LS = Louise Southerden; CS = Carlos Stewart; SIL = Struik Image Library; T/TP = Touchline/Tertius Pickard; IT = Ian Trafford; US = Universal Studios; WvR = Willem van Riet; VAP = Visual Addiction Photography; DW = David Wall; PW = Philip Wegener; WV = Whitewater Voyages; CW = Clive Williamson; ZP/JW = Zambezi Promotions/Julian Wentzel.

Key to locations: b = bottom; c = centre; l = left; r = right; t = top; tl = top left; tr = top right

Endpapers		JC	43		CS	87		ABl	124		PD
1		TB	44		JK	88		GB	125		NG/Michael Nichols
2-3		GI/TSI/Michael O'Leary	45		DH	90	l	DA	126		AB
4-5		ABl	46	l	JC	90	c	MS	127		GC
6-7		GI/TSI/John Running	46	c	GI/TSI/Harvey Kennan	90	r	GI/TSI/Glen Allison	128-129		HL
8-9		DE	46	r	ZB	91		DA	130		B&BD
12		GI/Mike Coppinger	47		TB	92		OK	131	t	PPL/PB
13		DD	48		LF	93		OK	131	b	LS
14	l	PD	50		SAP/TM	94		HL/Nick Haslam	132		HL/Maurice GG Harvey
14	c	Ax/Guy Marks	51		ZB	96	t, b	LG	133		AB
14	r	DA	52-53		ZB	97		LG	134	l, r	IT
15		TB	54		TB	98-99		MS	135		DW
16		source: Internet	55		TB	100		DE	136-137		IT
17		JJ	56		HL/T Moser	101		DE	138	l	JC
18		JJ	57		TB	102		DE	138	c	SIL/RDLH
19		DD	58		SAP/Chris Sharp	103		PW	138	r	GI/Peter Lillie
20		TB	59		TB	104	l	ABl	139		MN
21 (inset)		US	60-61		ZB	104	c	VAP/Ravi Miro Fry	140		GI/TSI/Sylvain Grandadam
21 (background)		DE	62-63		GI/TSI/Harvey Kennan	104	r	ABl			
22-23		ABl	64-65		TB	105		ABl	141		AF
25		ABl	66	l	ABl	106		ABl	142		DW
26	l	MN	66	c	AK	107		ABl	143		HL/Michael McIntyre
26	c	DB	66	r	MN	108	l, r	VAP/Ravi Miro Fry	144-145		GI/TSI/Chris Simpson
26	r	AH	67		ABl	109	tl, tr	VAP/Ravi Miro Fry	146		DW
27		DB	68		CW	109	b	ABl	147		MN
28 (background)		ZP/JW	69	l	CW	110-111		ABl	148-149		MN
29		GI/TSI/RGK Photogr.	69	r	GI/TSI/Dugald Bremner	112		JC	150		WvR
30		DB	70-71		ABl	113		JC	151		GA
31		KOB	72-73		ABl	114		DA	152		SIL
32-33		DB	74-75		ABl	116		DA	153		GA
34	l, c, r	DB	76		MN	117		AE	154		GI/Roger de la Harpe
35		TB	77		AK	118-119		DA	155		T/TP
36		WV	78-79		JC	120		ABl	156		DE
37	l	DB	80	l	AK	121		ABl	157		SIL/RDLH
37	r	MN	80-81		FM	122	l	IT	158-159		TB
38-39		BH	82-83		AK	122	c	DW	160		DD
40-41		DB	84-85		AK	122	r	MN			
42	l, r	TB	86		IG	123		MN			